THE MODERN WOODCUT

German : Early XV. Century. "The Madonna and Child" (Schreiber, 1058). $11\frac{1}{4} \times 7\frac{5}{8}$ in.

[2A]

THE MODERN WOODCUT

A STUDY OF THE EVOLUTION OF THE CRAFT
BY HERBERT FURST ('TIS') WITH A CHAPTER
ON THE PRACTICE OF XYLOGRAPHY BY
W. THOMAS SMITH WITH OVER TWO
HUNDRED ILLUSTRATIONS IN
BLACK & WHITE AND
SIXTEEN PLATES
IN COLOUR

JOHN LANE THE BODLEY HEAD LIMITED LONDON

FIRST PUBLISHED IN 1924

Made and Printed in Great Britain by
Lund, Humphries & Company, Limited
The Country Press, Bradford, England
and at *Three* Amen Corner
London, E.C.4

PREFACE

R. MALCOLM SALAMAN was good enough to bring Mrs. Raverat's woodcuts under my notice; they excited in me an interest in xylography as a means of free aesthetic expression. Mr. Salaman was thus the "first cause" of the following study and to him as the indefatigable champion of print makers I dedicate this book, though he is in no way responsible for the opinions I have expressed, the inferences and deductions I have made and the conclusions I have come to.

My thanks are also due to Mr. Campbell Dodgson, Mr. M. T. H. Sadler, Mr. R. A. Walker, Mr. John Lea, Mr. Frank Brangwyn, Mr. E. O. Hoppé and Mr. Léon de Smet for the kindness with which they have placed their valuable possessions at my disposal; to Mr. Laurence Binyon, Professor A. M. Hind, Professor A. W. Pollard, Mr. Martin Hardie, who have allowed me to consult them; to Mr. Huntly Carter, for interesting information about Russian art and permission to reproduce some of the material collected by him in Russia; to Messrs. H. W. Davies, of J. J. Leighton's, A. Zvemmer, successor to R. Jaeschke, Arthur Greatorex, Bromhead and Cutts, and "the XXI. Gallery," for information and help. Further, I am indebted to Signor Ettore Cozzani, the Editor of the Italian pioneer magazine "Eroica," for permission to reproduce some of its interesting contents; and to Mr. J. J. A. Murphy, who made himself responsible for a collection of the most characteristic American work and obtained the necessary permissions from the artists; to Mr. Ludovic Rodo, who helped me in a like manner, with regard to a number of French artists. Last, but not least, I wish to thank all those artists, both English and foreign, who freely consented to the reproduction of their work and so helped to give the book a more vital and immediate interest. In this connection and in fairness to the artists, it should be pointed out that it has been found impossible to do them in every case perfect justice so far as the illustrations are concerned. A compromise was inevitable if the price of the book was to remain at a reasonable figure. The difficulties are threefold. Without printing each colour reproduction separately and in the process most suitable for each case, it is impossible to produce entirely accurate results. Next, it has not been found practicable to keep the size of the illustrations to a uniform scale; some

B

V.

of the prints have had to be reduced so greatly, that the application of the same ratio of reduction to the smaller ones would have destroyed their purpose. Lastly, the technique employed by some artists, *e.g.*, Mr. Timothy Cole, is unsuitable for reproduction either by line or half-tone process, and to employ any other was, for reasons already stated, not feasible.

This the reader is asked to bear in mind, together with the fact that the intention of this study is to awaken curiosity about, and a general interest in, the significance of the *modern* woodcut, rather than to furnish a comprehensive history or iconography for the expert and the collector.

With reference to the chapter on " Hints on the Practice of Xylography," for which Mr. W. Thomas Smith is entirely responsible, it should be stated that Mr. Smith was asked by me to add it to my book as he is one of the now rapidly diminishing band of craftsmen who were properly apprenticed to wood engraving as a trade ; his thorough and practical knowledge of " the white line," coupled with his sympathy with creative design will, I hope, be found of value to artists who may wish to take up xylography as an additional means of expressing their emotions and thoughts.

November, 1923   HERBERT FURST

vi.

From T. Bewick's " Figures of British Landbirds."   Original size.   [30B]

CONTENTS

Page

vii.

LIST *of* ILLUSTRATIONS *in the* ALPHABETICAL ORDER OF THE NAMES OF THE ARTISTS

The figures in brackets denote the number of the illustration; the figures in black type the page on which they appear; the other figures the pages on which reference to them is made in the text. Anonymous cuts are mentioned under the name of the cutter's country. The nationality of the artist is indicated as follows: (A.) United States; (Au.) Austrian; (B.) Belgian; (Br.) British; (D.) Dutch; (Fl.) Flemish; (Fr.) French; (G.) German; (Gr.) Greek; (I.) Italian; (J.) Japanese; (N.) Norwegian; (P.) Polish; (R.) Russian; (S.) Swiss; (Sp.) Spanish. (*s*) denotes a cut on Soft wood; (*h*) a cut or engraving on Hard wood; (*l*) a Linoleum cut; *it has, however, not been possible to verify these designations in every case.*

x.

c

xiv.

xvi.

xvii.

xviii.

XX.

D

xxii.

THE MODERN WOODCUT

THE INTRODUCTION: POINTING OUT THE RELATION OF THE MODERN WOODCUT TO OUR OWN TIMES

THE "general reader," that faithful shadow of the equally insubstantial but perennially popular "man in the street," may well be forgiven if not a few of the illustrations which accompany the text of this book cause him, instead of pleasure, no more than sheer bewilderment.

The world, which, though few will believe it, includes also the "Art world," has passed and is still passing through a quick succession of curious phases; each apparently in violent opposition to its immediate predecessor and yet all linked together by the vital energies of organic growth.

Later ages will probably decide that humanity after an *infancy*— strictly speaking an incapacity of articulate utterance—of many aeons, came of age about the turn of the Twentieth Century, A.D., its adolescence having lasted from Aristotle to Darwin or thereabouts. What we are witnessing now, the clash of opinions and the clatter of more substantial things, is the outward sign of humanity's endeavour to settle down and to make itself at home in and on a sphere, the material extent of which it has only recently, that is within a child's memory, fully measured.

Man is at last becoming self-conscious : that is to say, trying to take an objective view of all things, and in particular, of their all-enwrapping envelope : his own Ego. In course of this attempt he is suffering many shocks, some of them violent, as might be expected. He is discovering on the one hand his limitations, on the other a hitherto unimagined and unimaginable increase of his potentialities. He may make mistakes, he may err ; he may sin ; innocent he is no longer. He cannot excuse himself with "The woman thou gavest me," nor she thrust the blame on the "beguiling serpent."

Mankind is learning to shoulder the responsibility of its own actions: it is about to take—within inevitable limitations—the control of its destiny. No wonder it is both restive and nervous.

This may sound a strange and grandiloquent sort of introduction to so humble a theme as "The Modern Woodcut." But the reader will find that its outstanding characteristics are self-consciousness and a sense of personal value, qualities strikingly absent from earlier stages. There is in all earlier work a trait of aesthetic innocence, a confiding trust in the absoluteness of its ideals, be these personified by a thousand goblins or a single God, or found in ancient creeds or " the new learning." To-day all this is gone : lost—I think irretrievably —to the modern artist.

The simplicity, the crudity even, that is apparent in so much modern work is in fact a manifestation of heightened complexity. To-day, the artist knows more consciously than ever before, that art consists in leaving out rather than in putting in ; he will, therefore, seek to do with one stroke as much as his immediate forbears did with a hundred.

But what distinguishes him, in common with all other truly modern workers, is that he feels himself the father of a potent future rather than the degenerate grandchild of a " glorious " past.

From Boccaccio's "De Claris Mulieribus." Published by Johann Zainer. Ulm, 1473. [5ᴮ]

xxviii.

From "Thérence en François." Published by Antoine Vérard, 1515. Original size. [17]

THE FIRST CHAPTER: DEFINING THE NATURE OF THE WOODCUT AND THE WOOD ENGRAVING WHICH TOGETHER CONSTITUTE THE CRAFT OF XYLOGRAPHY

NCE generally understood as a form of illustration, the term " cut " has all but lost its significance. Our grandfathers used the word to designate cheap prints and illustrations generally, and in this sense it still survives in the name of a weekly publication, popular with the errand boys and office boys, who thus helped its proprietor to a viscountcy and a Westminster funeral. *Habent sua fata.* . .

There is no doubt that, in the north of Europe at all events, wood was the cheapest and most convenient material employed for the pictorial sublimation and perpetuation of thought, and we, who use a germanic language, may enjoy the subtle relation of scriptures and pictures made manifest by etymology ; the *written book* being etymologically[1] a species of incised wood. To-day, the cheapest medium

[1]*Write*, Anglo-Saxon *writan* = to cut ; book, Anglo-Saxon *bóc* = beech. " The original ' books ' were pieces of writing on beechen board." SKEAT, CONCISE ETYMOL. DICT.

E

1

for the perpetuation, or rather for the multiplication, of both writing and picture making is metal, and the use of wood for pictorial purposes is due to other than purely economical reasons. What these reasons are is the problem we have set ourselves here to study. We must, therefore, first define the meaning of the term " Woodcut." There are now about the word " cut " what Sir Thomas Browne, to whom we owe its first use, would have called " bivious theorems and Janus faced doctrines "; so that a distinction is attempted between a woodcut and a wood engraving. That the difference between the two is not funda-mental will be clear when the methods which distinguish them are analysed. A woodcut, strictly speaking, is a print from a flat piece of soft wood, *e.g.*, beech, apple, pear or sycamore wood,[1] out of which the craftsman has carved a design, in such a manner that it may be inked and printed upon paper or other similar material. The carving is done with a small knife or a graver and a gouge, and in the following manner:[2] The craftsman either draws directly or traces an already existing drawing on the surface of a " plank " of wood, that is to say a board of about 7/8 inch thickness, sawn parallel with the grain and carefully planed. The cutter next makes his incisions along the lines of the drawing, so that after removal of the superfluous wood with knife or " scrive " and scorper, the design stands out raised from the ground and ready to be inked. A piece of suitable paper, previously moistened, is laid upon the inked surface, and subjected to pressure. The kind and degree of pressure depends on the nature of the design on and the nature of the paper, the harder and harsher the latter, the greater the pressure required.

This is a rough outline of the traditional method employed in the making of wood*cuts*.

The procedure in the case of wood *engraving* is very similar, with the following differences. The wood used is *hard* wood, generally boxwood, cut across the grain, not, as in the woodcut, with the grain. The surface, being on the endgrain of a dense wood, is very much firmer, and enables the engraver to use a different set of tools, namely, in addition to the scorpers, and instead of the knife: gravers, tint tools and " spit stickers " (a tool with a slightly convex cutting edge), and the threading tool, which produces a series of parallel lines. The object of these different tools is to enable the craftsman to vary not only the

[1] Both Linoleum and Rubber are occasionally used as substitutes for soft wood ; the resulting prints do not differ from soft-wood cuts necessarily sufficiently to make such differences as exist unmistakable.

[2] For practical instructions in the craft, the reader is referred to Mr. Thomas Smith's chapter at the end of the book.

2

German; Early XV. Century: "St. Jerome" (Schreiber, 1546). 7⅞×5 in. [2B]

width but the character of his lines, and to cover surfaces of even tone more quickly.

The main difference, however, between the cut and the engraving is in the cutting action, which, in the case of the knife, is towards, and in the case of the graver, is away from, the body. It must be noted that, nevertheless, some craftsmen use the knife on the hard wood, and the graver,[1] or "scrive," has always been used in connection with soft wood so that, if for no other reason, a hard and fast distinction cannot be made. But there is another reason which makes it preferable to regard both methods as one : it is this, that the problem is fundamentally the same, *viz* : the production of a print from a *relief-*block of wood; that is to say, from a block of wood so cut that its *surface* will print the design, exactly as is the case with a rubber stamp. It is, in fact, a stamping process,[2] and the printing has to be done with a vertical pressure, which may be applied either through the ordinary printing press or, as is the case with all the engravers' or cutters' *proofs*, by hand through the means of a burnisher, a brush, a roller, or even the finger-nail or the sole of the foot.

As regards the printing, the following observations have to be made. Woodcuts proper, *i.e.*, those cut on the plank of soft wood can, and often do, show the grain of the wood in printing, a quality much exploited by the Japanese and also to some extent by European artists. Wood engravings printed from hard wood show no grain, but occasionally white lines that cut across the design. These are caused by the fact that it is impossible to make boxwood blocks of any considerable size; a nine inch block, such as one of Bewick's, preserved in the British Museum, is now hardly procurable. The modern blocks are composed of small squares not exceeding one or two square inches very greatly. These small blocks are glued together and "keyed" together to make larger surfaces and it happens, either when the wood is not properly seasoned or when the printing press is not properly geared that the joints separate, causing the white lines to appear in the print. Such seams occur frequently also in composite woodcuts on soft wood. Described in this manner the method of producing prints from wood would appear to be a very simple matter, but this description has not touched upon the main problem, which is the method and the quality of design ; a great deal, everything in fact, depends upon this.

I would emphasize the *method* of design, and not the word design

[1] Dürer called it " Eiselein "—little iron—not " Messer," *i.e.*, knife.
[2] Amongst Sir Aurel Stein's collection of ninth century Buddhist woodcuts at the British Museum, sheets of such stamped woodcuts impressions may be seen.

3

only, which is generally and quite wrongly stressed, because it inevitably leads to a misunderstanding. The design in itself is not always and, as we shall see, not necessarily a criterion at all.

Let us, first, visualize the difference between xylography (a term I will use as including wood cutting as well as wood engraving), and other multiplying processes.

The simplest of these latter is lithography, because, in the first place, it requires no special tool. The lithographer can draw on the stone (or its substitutes) either with chalk (lithographic) or with the pen or with the brush ; he can also use a knife to scrape, or a needle to scratch his drawing if he wishes to break or lighten his tones. Lithography is based on the antipathy between grease and water. The lithographic stone is, naturally, aluminium or zinc, as substitutes are, artificially, so constituted that they will greedily absorb both water and grease. The lithographic chalk is like the lithographic ink, greasy. It follows that the lithographic surface where it has been first touched by the greasy chalk and subsequently soaked in water, rejects the grease on its moistened surface and holds the ink on its greased surface. A sheet of paper laid upon the stone (or its substitute) will be imprinted, under pressure with the ink that has been held by the parts of the stone which have been drawn upon.

With the exception of the fixing of the drawing by acids, there is, therefore, no kind of " process," and the actual drawing presents hardly more difficulties to the artist than a drawing on paper.

The lithograph, like the xylograph, is a *surface* print.

The " dry point " and the etching are like engravings on metal " intaglio " prints, that is to say, the ink instead of being picked up from the surface, is pressed on to the paper from the grooves made by the tools or the acid. It follows that whilst it is possible both in xylography and in lithography to print blacks (or any other colour for that matter) in masses, it is only possible to print blacks from the etched and the engraved plate (dry-point is a species of engraving) in lines.[1] Here then, is the great distinction between the wood and stone on the one hand and the cited metal processes on the other. It means that in engraving, in etching and dry point, the artist has to limit his method of design severely to such forms as are expressible by lines or parts of lines—*i.e.*, dots. In mezzotint and aquatint, on the other hand, the mechanical disability consists in the fact that these

[1]There are, it is true, also soft metal cuts which resemble the woodcut, but they are not capable of producing black masses of the richness which distinguishes the wood block.

4

Early Flemish, about 1450.   From a Block Book : " Biblia Pauperum."   Original size.   [5]

5

processes, the nature of which we need not discuss here, cannot in themselves express lines at all.

It is clear then that each process, except the lithographic one perhaps, imposes upon the craftsman a limitation on which his *method* as distinct from the *nature* of his design must be based.

Xylography imposes upon the craftsman's hand perhaps a greater number of limitations than any of the other multiplying processes. To begin with his material is *wooden*, even in the metaphorical sense of the word ; it is not ingratiating ; it speaks naturally only in black and white ; it has no half-tones. It can be forced to render half-tones only in two ways. One of these consists in lowering the level of the parts which are to print grey, so that they will not receive so much ink and will not be subjected to so much pressure. The other method is to break up the blacks by a system of lines or dots. The planning of this linear convention can be approached from two opposite directions. The first and simplest approach was, historically, discovered or at least exploited last. It starts from the premise that the wood block, uncut, prints a solid black (or any other colour). Therefore, to draw on it, it is only necessary to cut grooves into the block which will print as white lines. The nature, width and number of these white lines will determine the nature, character and quality of the design. The other less practical method and the less *natural* one, but which, requiring less forethought in cutting, came, for that reason, first into use, is to regard the block as if it were like a sheet of *white* paper upon which the design has to be drawn in *black* in order to produce the " picture." The craftsman in this case transfers his drawing to the wood block and removes all those parts of the wood which are not drawn upon ; his half-tones are made by preserving the black lines and rendering shading by hatching or cross hatching of these lines.When it is considered that at least eight manipulations of the knife are necessary to make a single black line in this manner it will be realized how tedious and cumbersome this approach becomes.

It will be appreciated that the method of design in xylography must also be affected by the character of the material, *i.e.*, the wood itself in which the design is made. This method will, however, be still further modified by the tools with which the design is effected.

Whilst there is no kinship between the tools of lithography—chalk, pen or brush—and the xylographic tools, there is a certain amount of kinship between the latter and the graver and the " needle," of the metal engraver and " dry point etcher " (wrongly so called because he

6

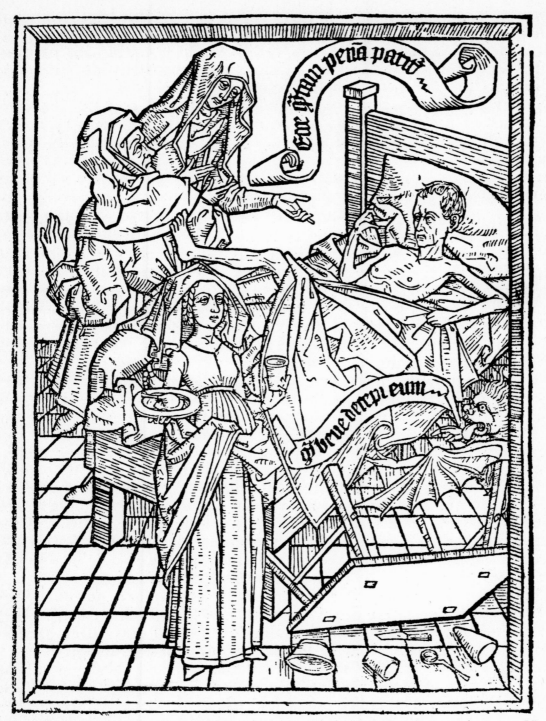

Early Flemish, about 1450.   From a Block Book : " Ars Moriendi."   Original size.   [6]

uses no etching fluid). In all these cases the tool is driven with more or less force into the surface of the material from which a physical restraint of varying degree on the freedom of the line naturally results, a restraint which the draughtsman, the painter and the etcher experience hardly if at all.

Now let us see how the method of designing due to the nature of xylography influences the *nature* of the design.

We will begin with the method which came chronologically first : the black line.

Since the craftsman intending to use the black line regards the block as if it were a sheet of white paper, his problem is to remove all that part of the surface which is not to print—*i.e.*, the greater part. The primitive craftsman drew—either with a lead point or a reed pen, or possibly, as in the East, with brush and ink—his black line design on the block. He then severed the outlines from the main surface, which he removed with a gouge or scorper, when the " picture " would stand out in relief ready to be inked and printed from. The nature of the design would be that of a very coarse outline drawing, seemingly done with pen or pencil, but actually modified by the nature of material and tools and the degree of the cutter's skill.

The next aim of the craftsman, and this applies to the primitive as well as the modern beginner, would be to *suppress* the evidence of the tool by meticulous preservation of the drawn lines, and with increasing dexterity he would be tempted to cut more and more ambitious drawings in which a freer rein would be given to pen or pencil. Shading would be attempted first by a simple method of parallel hatching, next by cross hatching. Since, however, a system of shading by lines of necessity brings a number of black lines close together the craftsman would early discover that by using a scrive, instead of the knife, he could do with a single movement of the tool what would require a quadruple application of the knife—and his black lines would result virtually from the cutting of intersticial *white* lines.

This method would bring his prints in appearance nearer to the linear convention of the metal engraver, and the woodcut, after having effaced itself in order to *imitate* a drawing, would now efface itself in order to *become something in the nature of metal* engraving.

There is, however, also another evolution from the black line. The first purpose of the woodcut was essentially a substitution of the painted picture. The craftsman would use his lines as outlines for the colours applied by hand. By a simple association of ideas he would

8

Erhard Reuwich, 1486.   Frontispiece to Breydenbach's " Pilgrimage to Jerusalem."   Published
at Mainz. $10\frac{3}{4} \times 7\frac{1}{2}$ in. [7]

discover the use of a colour block which would add, after being inked all over, at least one tone or colour to the black and white print. Proceeding further by simple stages he would add more blocks in order to produce more colours, and find that simple excisions of the surface of the "tone" block would give the effect of *high* lights in imitation of drawings *heightened* with white.

The woodcutter would now be well on the way to discovering the woodcut in colour and other complex processes of to-day.

Thus the black line method keeps the woodprint from beginning to end in a servile reproductive state, the onus of design falling all along on the original designer, whether he be identical with the cutter or not. The problem of the designer in white line is an entirely different one, requiring for its solution more forethought even than that which the black line designer may impose upon himself.

From purely associative causes white is in design the equivalent of light and black the equivalent of shade. Consequently, the white line incised upon the wood block will tell as a light value, whether it is intended to do so or not. If the cutter takes no notice of this fact he will get results similar to the rubbings taken from engraved stones, or to the rare and curious " Teigdrucke " or paste prints.[1] The effect of these is that of a negative, and only negative results can be obtained by such means unless the cutter takes the (black) surface of his block into consideration as an integral, and, as it were, already existing part of his design. This means, in other words, that in devising the shape and function of the white line he cuts he must consider the shape and function of the black surface the excision leaves behind. To have done this—albeit in the technique of the metal engraver—is Bewick's great merit—but his achievement was exploited by engravers and reproducers who *thought* in black line, and did so of necessity, since the drawings or paintings they " interpreted " were for the most part conceived in the traditional contour line of the Old Masters. Creative exploitation of the white line became possible only after the Impressionists had accustomed the artist's eye not only to *think* in light values—but also to draw in that sense.

The white line cut, therefore, which always has required more intelligence in its application, is the natural method of the creative artist, and as such, used by the truly modern woodcutter, whether as a light or as colour value, whether for its plastic or its decorative worth.

[1] " Generally a glutinous ink (paste) was used, so that gold leaf could be attached and further hints of colour were sometimes added to the impressions." A Guide to the Processes and Schools of Engraving, etc   British Museum publication, 1914.

10

THE SECOND CHAPTER: GIVING A SHORT SURVEY OF THE HISTORY OF THE WOODCUT FROM THE EARLIEST KNOWN EXAMPLE TO THE COMMENCEMENT OF THE NINETEENTH CENTURY

"THE earliest woodcut known in the world at present" Mr. Laurence Binyon states,¹ is the Frontispiece to the Chinese text of a Sanscrit book " The Diamond Sutra." It is dated "the ninth year of Hsien-t'ung, *i.e.*, 868 A.D.," and represents " The Buddha discoursing to Subhuti," his aged disciple [1]. Far from being primitive in execution, this crowded design is cut with great skill in simple black line facsimile, and more expertly than some much later work. Chinese woodcuts were, however, produced not only as book illustrations, but " probably in great masses as aids to popular devotion and as cheap substitutes for religious paintings."

Precisely the same is true of the use which this craft was first put to, although at a much later date, in Europe. Woodcuts were distributed in quantities amongst the faithful as mementos of religious festivals and pilgrimages; they were also sent as New Year greetings. In addition to this, however, they served to decorate the insides of bookcovers, the lids of offertory boxes; they were used for calendars and almanacs; and the playing-card makers formed a separate branch of the craft. Furthermore, printed in large composite sheets, the woodcut served the purpose of mural paintings and, eventually, the humbler purposes of the paperhanger and cotton printer.

The earliest specimens of the pictorial woodcut in Europe only take us back to the threshold of the fifteenth century. It is useless to pretend that the majority of such prints have much aesthetic value. In every age the bulk of aesthetic manufacture is more or less insignificant. Nevertheless, in the case of these early woodcuts, there are a considerable number of exceptions [2A], and this at least should be said, that even the indifferent cuts of the earlier periods are aesthetically more justifiable than the average of the later and technically more accomplished productions. As none of the earlier prints are associated with the names of known artists or craftsmen an enumeration of the more remarkable ones,

¹" Catalogue of Japanese and Chinese woodcuts preserved in the British Museum."

without accompanying illustrations, would here hardly serve a useful purpose. Good collections of originals and reproductions are to be seen in most of the public print cabinets of Europe.

The transition from the single sheet pictorial woodcut to the printed book illustration is represented by the so-called block books. These were books made up of single sheets printed from wooden " blocks " on which not only the picture, but also the text was cut. There are such books in which the pictorial part is printed and the text inserted in manuscript, but it does not follow that such books were necessarily the earlier ones ; nor indeed that block books are always earlier than those printed after Gutenberg's invention of movable type. Block books vary in quality immensely, but in the best examples show a high degree of characterization, and a nice feeling for architectural composition. They are generally printed in a pale ink and were intended for hand colouring. Amongst the most celebrated block books the following may be mentioned : the "Apocalypse," of Netherlandish origin, *circa* 1430; the " Biblia Pauperum," [5] a handbook for the poorer clergy, about the same date, and the "Ars Moriendi," [6] of about 1450, of which the first edition is in the British Museum. Two other well-known block books are the " Historia beatae Virginis ex cantico canticorum " and the " Speculum humanae salvationis," both *circa* 1460 in their first editions. Altogether there are about thirty block books and one hundred editions known. Their characteristic is the deep impression caused by rubbing the paper down on the block, so that its edges show in relief on the back.

The woodcut as a book illustration, as we understand the term to-day, begins soon after the establishment of the printing press. The earliest books were, except for initials, not illustrated ; and where illustrations appear their object is rather to deceive the unwary into the belief that they were acquiring *hand-painted* illuminated manuscripts. We shall revert to this point presently.

Albrecht Pfister, of Bamberg, is credited with the first issue of illustrated books—at the beginning of the fourteen sixties, amongst them a Latin and a German edition of the " Biblia Pauperum." After a lapse of several years, the publication of illustrated books suddenly burst forth with incredible vigour from 1470 onwards.

Printing presses were established not only in Germany, but in Italy and France, and in the Netherlands by the Germans. Individual towns, with individual rather than national characteristics, thus became centres of civilization. In Germany—Ulm, Augsburg, Nuremburg,

12

From the Chinese woodcut, A.D. 868: "The Buddha discoursing to Subhuti." Illustration for the Chinese Translation of the "Diamond Sutra." "The earliest woodcut known." [1]

Wanden Surianen woenende the iΘerusalem ende.in die landen die segghen hem seluen kersten menschen te wesen

Eck sijn noch te Iberusalem sommighe andere menschen ghe= noemt suriani van die stadt sur die hieruoirmaels een machti= ghe stadt was als die sommighe segghen Offte sij werden ghe= noemt Suriani van dat lantscap van Syrien van welcken sij oeck Syri ghenoemt werden Dese woenē in den oesten onder verscheyden co ninghen eñ vorsten offte princen sarracenē ende barbaren onder welck sij van voirtijts verdruct werden mit bedwanck des dienstes offte eyghen= scaps altoes staende onder tribuut eñ eyghenscap Het sijn gheen strijd= bare luden heel ombequaem ten oirloghe zeer beanxt eñ verueert.sij ghe bruken gheen boghen offte enich schut als andere menschen. Mer sij sijn well ghestelt tot bouwerck eñ andere zware arbeyt Sij syn oeck int me= ste deel ongheloüighe ketthers bedriegghelick valsch ende loghenachtich. aen hanghende die auentuer eñ zeer bereit tot ghiften eñ gaue te ontfan ghen Stelenlen rouen houden sy als voir niet eñ voir gheen sunde Sij openbaren die heymelicheiden der kersten verradelick totte onghelouighē heyden eñ den sarracenē onder welck sij opgheuoedt eñ ghemeghhet hoirre quade wercken mede gekeert hebben Sij houden mit groter neersticheit hoir wijuē besloten ghelijcken als die sarracenē.eñ sy laten hoir wijuen offte hoir dochteren int openbair niet wt gaen dan bedect mit linnēlake= nen eñ hoir aensichterē voirdect mit zwart laken op dat sij van nyemāt ghesien sellen werden Sij bewarē so scherpelic hoir dochterē dat sij niet

p ij

A page from Reuwich's "Pilgrimage to Jerusalem." Mainz, 1486. Original size. [8]

13

From "Discours du Songe de Poliphile," designed and cut by Jean Cousins (?) for Jacques Kerver, Paris, 1554. [13]

Strassburg, Basle, Mainz, Cologne, Wittenberg, Lubeck, lead the way ; in Italy—Venice, Verona, Florence, Rome, Ferrara ; in France—Paris and Lyons ; in the Netherlands—Louvain, Delft, Utrecht, Gouda, Haarlem, the Flemish activities being finally all absorbed by Antwerp, which became the centre of the entire Netherlandish printing trade.

The subject matter of these books which mark the arrival of humanistic culture was no longer primarily religious. Pfister's first illustrated book, 1461, *viz.*, Boner's " Edelstein " was a collection of Fables. Boccaccio's " De claris mulieribus " was, both in Latin and German, a favourite of the period ; Æsop's Fables, always henceforth popular with woodcut illustrators, appear as early as 1476 in Ulm, an Italian edition three years later in Verona, and another one in Naples in 1489, earlier than the famous Florentine book illustrators began their work. Books of

14

POLIPHILO QVIVI NARRA, CHE GLI PARVE AN‐
CORA DI DORMIRE, ET ALTRONDE IN SOMNO
RITROVARSE IN VNA CONVALLE, LA QVALE NEL
FINE ERA SERATA DE VNA MIRABILE CLAVSVRA
CVM VNA PORTENTOSA PYRAMIDE, DE ADMI‐
RATIONE DIGNA, ET VNO EXCELSO OBELISCO DE
SOPRA. LA QVALE CVM DILIGENTIA ET PIACERE
SVBTILMENTE LA CONSIDEROE.

L A SPAVENTEVOLE SILVA, ET CONSTI‐
pato Nemore euaso, & gli primi altri lochi per el dolce
somno che se haueua per le fesse & prosternate mébre dif‐
fuso relicti, me ritrouai di nouo in uno piu delectabile
sito assai piu che el præcedente. Elquale non era de mon‐
ti horridi, & crepidinose rupe intorniato, ne falcato di
strumosi iugi. Ma compositamente de grate montagniole di non tro‐
po altecia. Siluose di giouani quercioli, di roburi, fraxini & Carpi‐
ni, & di frondosi Esculi, & Ilice, & di teneri Coryli, & di Alni, & di Ti‐
lie, & di Opio, & de infructuosi Oleastri, dispositi secondo laspecto de
gli arboriferi Colli. Et giu al piano erano grate siluule di altri siluatici

A page from the " Hypnerotomachia Poliphili," printed by Aldus Manutius, Venice,
1499. 8⅝ × 6¼ in.

[12]

15

travel, such as " Mandeville's Journey to Jerusalem " appear in a German translation at Augsburg in 1481, and Breydenbach's " Peregrinationes in Montem Syon," a " Pilgrimage to the Holy City "[7, 8] five years later, at Mainz. An illustrated edition of Dante's " Divina Comedia " is published in Venice in 1491; a medical book, Kelham's "Fasciculus Medicinae " in 1493. The most famous illustrated Italian book of this period, a novel entitled the " Hypnerotomachia Poliphili," [12] which has had a great influence on modern book illustration and book-" building " generally, was issued by Aldus Manutius, at Venice, in 1499.

Thus by the commencement of the sixteenth century, the woodcut illustrator was able to try his hand at and apply his ingenuity to every variety of subject matter, from the religious to the scientific, from the most fantastic to the most prosaic. Life, hitherto on the whole only a pilgrimage through the Vale of Tears, in which the highest art one could acquire was the "Ars Moriendi "—the art of dying—became suddenly " the great adventure." The flight of imagination which had fixed man's eyes, not so much on the stars as on the glory of heaven and the tortures of hell, ceases. Man comes down to earth. This coming down to concrete realities, or perhaps better expressed to realities which are visualized and represented as if they had a concrete existence, is mirrored by the work of that artist whose reputation as a woodcutter stands highest, whose influence was for a long time greatest, and of whom it is yet doubtful how much actual " woodcutting " he ever did, Dürer. That such a doubt can exist is both natural and characteristic for the turn the craft took from Dürer's day and for a long time onward.

Dürer, one of the profoundest artists of his period, and much more than a mere craftsman, was as a painter, nevertheless, surpassed by the Italians and even by his younger compatriot Holbein; yet there is no one, either before him or since, who has equalled him in invention or conception as a poet of the drawn line, if we qualify this claim by the word *literary*. Designs of an aesthetic simplicity such as his " St. Christopher " [19] or his " Samson " are exceptional. Dürer's woodcuts, even more than his engravings, must almost without exception be *read* [18] to be enjoyed, a qualification which shall be explained presently. Here let us note that Dürer's magnificent series of the "Apocalypse " marks the beginning of what is generally recognized as Dürer's style. It contains fifteen single sheets published in 1498, with a sixteenth added to the second edition issued in 1511. In this series the artist's

16

Albrecht Dürer, The Four Horsemen from the "Apocalypse," 1498. 15 × 11 in.   [18]

imagination twines itself like a passion flower round the words of the evangelist, revealing his inexhaustible courage in attempting to visualize the darkly turbulent imagery of the book. At the same time the artist began his series of the so-called " Great Passion," of which the complete series of twelve was not issued until 1511, which year also saw the publication of the " Little Passion," a series of thirty-seven prints only begun in 1520. In the same year another series, begun in 1504, also made its appearance, " The Life of Mary," which is at once the least austere and the most popular of all his work. Virtually an " idyll " on family life and home happiness, it shows the master's human rather than the brooding philosophic side of his character.

Dürer designed a number of separate cuts, portraits, of which " Eobanus Hesse " deserves special mention ; religious subjects, of which the " Last Supper " of 1523 was one of the best, and he also took part in Emperor Maximilian's gigantic but ill-conceived woodcut enterprises, the " Arch of Triumph " and the " Triumphal Procession."

Amongst the most important of Dürer's followers were Hans Leonhard Schäuffelein, Hans Sebald Beham and Hans Baldung Grien, the latter gifted with an extraordinary power and unusual trend of imagination which he probably owes more to that strange genius, the painter Matthias Gruenewald, whom we may acclaim as an early " expressionist." Grien's aesthetic language expressed itself mainly in the human figure, but his "Fighting Horses"[22] have been a source of inspiration to modern expressionists.

A contrast to Grien's is the work of Albrecht Altdorffer. Equally remarkable as one of the first painters and designers of pure landscape and as a most delicate and skilful maker of woodcuts, he was also the first to print the woodcut in many colours.

Hans Burgkmair, associated with Dürer in the Emperor's employ, for whom he designed nearly the whole of the " Triumphal Procession " and the incomplete "Weiss Kunig," was an artist whose talents were particularly fit for the translation of the Italian Renaissance Spirit into German diction. He must be noted here as one of the first designers for the woodcut in colour. His equestrian portrait of Emperor Maximilian appeared in 1508, but the actual colour printing—black line and a red tone block with heightening in gold—was due to his woodcutter, Jobst de Negker. This manner of producing colour prints was preceded by another famous woodcut designer's invention, or at least practice, of " heightening " the prints with gold and silver—a block with an adhesive substance being imprinted on the line block and the gold

18

Albrecht Dürer: "St. Christopher." 1511. 8¼ × 8¼ in.

dusted upon it subsequently. This artist was Lucas Cranach, in his best works, for instance a standing figure of St. George, and the adoration of the Heart of Jesus, second only to Dürer.

As an illustrator Hans Holbein stands head and shoulders above all his contemporaries, Dürer not excluded. There was indeed no one in any country to equal him, not so much for depth of feeling or imagination, but for clearness of expression. Many of his designs were cut in metal, some of them in both metal and wood. His greatest works in woodcut are the Old Testament illustrations and the so-called "Dance of Death," which was a spirited satire and socialistic comment on life rather than the morbid expression of dogmatic faith. The "Dance of Death" cuts [21], though designed between 1523 and 1526, were not published until 1538, that is to say at the same time as the Old Testament illustrations, and they were issued in Lyons, not in Basle where they had been designed, nor in England where the artist had settled in 1532. But Holbein did design the title page of Miles Coverdale's first Bible in English, and also several cuts for Cranmer's Catechism. What might be regarded as an obstacle to success proved in Holbein's case an advantage; unlike Dürer he was not his own publisher, but had to submit to the requirements of publishers, not only as to size, but also as to style and subject. Based on the woodcuts of the Venetian

Detail of Page from the "Malermi" Bible, opposite.
Original size.   [11]

Malermi Bible [10, 11], his style developed something of Italian simplicity and clarity of expression; but to this he added Teutonic depth of sentiment. The requirements of book building, the artist's aesthetic appreciation of the printed page as a whole, rather than of the individual design, constitutes Holbein's style, which influenced the book illustrators of France more than his own compatriots.

What we appreciate in these illustrations of Holbein's and in the work that came after, has, however, very little to do with the woodcut as such, and the further we recede from the end of the fifteenth century and the nearer we approach to the nineteenth century the less does the material count. Holbein was fortunate in having a craftsman such as Hans Lützelburger for a cutter; without a skilful craftsman the value of the design would have been lost. On the other hand, with an absolutely faithful method of reproduction, even though it were entirely

20

appreſo a uno arbore per capilli morite: & morto
lui Dauid recupero el regno:& la terra.& coſeque-
temente regno i pace:& alhora dauid feceqſto pſal
mo & e claro qſto titulo cioe pſalmo de dauid: qua
do fuli reſtituita la terra. etcet.   XCVI.

L ſignor ha regnato:ralegraſi la terra ſe
ralegraráno le molte iſule.Intorno a lui
e la nube & obſcurita:la iuſtitia & iudi
cio ſaranno caſtigamento dela ſua ſedia.
Dináci a lui andara el fuoco:&bruſara linimici ſuoi
ditorno a lui.Reſplédetero le fulgura ſua al circui-
ro d la terra:uid la terra & fu comoſa.Coe cera ſe ſq
gliorono i môti dala faccia dl ſignor:dala ſacia dl ſi
gnor ogni terra.Racotorono i cieli la iuſtitia ſua:&
uidero tutti i populi la gloria ſua.Siano coſuſi tutti
cb adorano lydola ſculpiti:& qlli che ſe gloriano ne
li falſi dei ſuoi:Adoratilo tutti uoi angeli ſuoi:ſyon
halo udito & e ſatta lieta.Et alegranſi gli figlioli de
iuda:o ſignor per gli iudicii tuoi.Perho che tu ſei al
tiſſimo ſignor ſopra ogni terra: molto ſei exaltato
ſopra tutti i dei. Voi che amate el ſignore:habiate
in odio el male:el ſignor guarda lanime de ſuoi ſan
cti ne la mano del peccatore liberara quelli.Naſciu
to e la luce al iuſto:& la leticia a i dritti del cuor.
Ralegratiue iuſti nel ſignore:confeſſatiue alla me-
moria de la ſanctificatione ſua.Amen.   Titulo.
           Pſalmo de Dauid.
La expoſitione de queſto titulo piu uolte e ſtata
dimoſtrata:& de la materia del pſalmo:glie da ſape
re che ſono doe coſe che ſerua lhuomo da la uolun
ta de pregare:& iducelo al bene dela uirtu: cioe lamore dela gloria:& el timor de la pena.Vnde el ti-
more dela pena retrahe lhomo dal male:ma lamore
dela gloria induce al bene:Et queſte doe coſe ſe cau
ſano i noi:per coſideratione de i duo auenimenti de
chriſto:cioe del auenimento de chriſto che e ſtato i
queſto mondo:& del auenimento al di del iudicio.
Diche el pſalmiſta uolendoci tirare al amore: & al
timor de dio tracta in queſto pſalmo de luno & lal
tro auenimento de chriſto.etcetera.   XCVII.

Antate al ſignor el nouo canto: pche le
merauegUe ha fatto: Egli ha ſe ſaluato
co la ſuo dextra:& el braccio ſancto ſuo
Ha manifeſtato el ſignor el ſuo ſaluator
nel coſpecto dele gete ha reuelato la iuſtitia ſua.Ha
ſe arecordato dela ſua miſericordia & uerita:& dela
caſa de iſrael.Videro tutti li termini de la tetra:el ſal
uator del dio noſtro.Iubilate a dio ogni terra:cáta-
te ralegratiue:& pſalmizate.Lodate el ſignor ne la

cythara:colla uoce del pſalmo:con tube battute:&
co uoce de tuba cornea.Iubilate al ſignor nel coſpe
cto del re:mouaſi el mare:& la ſua plenitudine el cir
cuito de la terra:& ogniuno che habita in eſſa.Faci
no feſta co mane i ſiumi,iſieme i môti ſe legrarano
dala faccia del ſignor iperho che glie uenuto a iudi
care la terra:Iudicara el circuito de la terra:nela iuſti
cia & i populi nela equita.Amen.   Titulo:
        Pſalmo de dauid:
Queſto pſalmo non e ſondato ſopra alcüa hiſto
ria:auenga che ſecodo gli hebrei: & maxime Rabi
Salomone:dice come dauid fece queſto pſalmo pro
phetizando del re meſias:& del ſuo regno:ma loro
itendendo del regno temporale:& e uero chel pſal
mo e apropriato a chriſto uero meſſia:& del ſuo regno ſpirituale:& eterno & amaeſtrace cb adoriamo
el uero dio:& uero re:etcetera.   XCVIII:

Diráſi i populi pcb:el ſignor ha rgnato:
mouaſi la terra pche tu ſedi ſopra li che
rubini.El ſignor e grade i ſyo:& e excel
ſo ſopra tutti i populi. Cofeſſino al tuo
nome grade:pche eglie terribile & ſacto: & lhonor
del re ama el iudicio:tu pparaſti le directioe i iacob
tu feceſti el iudicio & la iuſticia. Exaltate el ſignor
dio nfo adorate el ſcabello di ſuoi piedi:ipho cbgli
e ſancto.Moyſes & aaro fuorono ne ſuoi ſacerdoti
& ſamuel tra color che iuocao el nome ſuo.Inuoca
no el ſignor & lui gli exaudiua:ne la colona: de nube a lor parlaua.Obſeruauano li ſuoi teſtimonii: &
el comádaméto che dicde a qlli.Signor dio nro tu
li exaudiui:dio tu foſti beniuolo & uidicatore in
tutte lor itentioe.Exaltate el ſignor dio nfo.& ado
rate nel mote ſacto ſuo:pho che glie ſacto el ſignor
dio nfo.Amé: Titulo. Pſalmo ne la coſeſſioe.
Queſto pſalmo no e ſodato ſopra alcua hiſtoria:
ma tracta dela coſeſſioe,e adunq el ſentiméto del
titulo:pſalmo dela coſeſſione cioe qſto pſalmo tra
cta de doe coſeſſioe:cioe coſeſſioe dela laude:& con
feſſioe dela colpa.Vnde la itentione del pſalmiſta e
iducere li pfecti a laudare dio.& gli peccatori a con
feſſare lor peccati:& defecti:etcetera.   XCIX

Vbilate a dio ogni terra:al ſignor ſerui-
te in alegreza.Intrate nel conſpecto ſuo
ne la legreza. Sapiate come el ſignore e
dio:egli ne ha fatto non noi ce faciamo
Voi che ſete populo ſuo:& pecore dela ſua paſtura
intrate nele ſue porte & confeſſione:ne ſuoi porti-
ci in laude a confeſſare a lui. Laudate el nome ſuo
perche ſuaue e el ſignor in eterno e la ſna miſericor
dia:& infino nela generatione : & la generatioe e la
uerita ſua.Amé.   Titulo. Pſalmo de dauid.
Queſto pſalmo e attribuito a Dauid. Et quanto
alla littera glie da ſapere come Dauid quando dop
po molte perſecutione ſe uide eſſere da Dio libera-
to & ſublimato al regno come ſe lege nel ſecondo
di re al.v.capitulo.Alhora Dauid ſe diſpoſe firma-
méte nel ſuo cuore de bene uſare la regia potétia.&
pcb ſon doe ſpeciale uirtu regie coe la miſericordia
& iuſticia:come dice yſidoro ne le ethimologie ſue
al nono:& pho ſe diſpoſe coſeruare nel ſuo cuor q
ſte doe uirtu acio che a boni ſuoſſe piatoſo & miſe-

A page from the "Malermi" Bible, an Italian Translation printed at Venice by Lucantonio
Giunta, 1490. 9¾ × 6⅜ in.   [10]

Hans Baldung Grien: " Fighting Horses." 1534. $8\frac{3}{8} \times 12\frac{5}{8}$ in.

mechanical, it is conceivable that Holbein's designs might have been superior Lützelburger's cuts. It is, as I say, conceivable. Nevertheless, we must grant that the peculiar attractiveness of such a series as the " Dance of Death " is, apart from the treatment of the subject, due to the manner in which the artist designed *for* the woodcutter. But in this way our appreciation is divided against itself, for we have to separate the design from the cut, and if we were to pursue this plan we should find ourselves analysing either the history of creative design or the histories of the various reproductive methods ; neither of which investigations are germane to the purpose of this book. Suffice it here to say that the culmination which the woodcut found under Dürer and Holbein, neither of whom practiced the craft to any extent, if at all, led immediately to its downfall as a form of *creative* art. Henceforth and until the last, the nineteenth century, no artist of the first rank had anything to do with it, with perhaps the exception of Titian, whose bold pen drawings were cut in wood by Niccolo Boldrini and others, and of Rubens, who found in Christopher Jegher

22

Der Edelman.

From Holbein's " Dance of Death." 1538. Designed between
1523 and 1526. Cut by H. Lützelburger. Original size. [21]

an apt and able interpreter of his fleshy, subtle and penetrating virility. But however skilful the cutting, and some wonderful performances (such as the portrait-cut of Fr. Priscianesi, from a book " Della Lingua romana," Venice, 1540) were made in the later years of the sixteenth century in Italy and France, the woodcut was no longer expressive except of some *outside* quality—be it that of drawing, painting or metal engraving. Ugo da Carpi had in the early sixteenth century introduced his method of Chiaroscuro cutting [23] by which he produced interpretative reproductions of Raphael's and other masters' drawings, and in the seventeenth century Christopher Jegher won, as we have just said, Rubens' aid and appreciation in his—as such remarkable—efforts to interpret the master's qualities in black and white, but these qualities were got by methods of the line engraver adapted to the relief technique of wood [26].

The acme of the craft in the eighteenth century is represented by Papillon's, the French woodcutter's, page ornaments [29], vignettes and head pieces cut with great skill in the manner of copperplate engravings. The work of this kind done in other countries was negligible. The wood had effectually ceased to be the mouthpiece of its own messages.

Towards the end of the eighteenth century Thomas Bewick, by adopting a new technique, [30, 30B] based nevertheless on the metal engraver's, gave the old craft a new lease of life. His illustrations of natural history books, the " General History of Quadrupeds "—published in 1790—ushered in a new era. Some of his animals were fantastic enough for the sixteenth century, but the method in which the blocks were cut was his own. Much better and far more attractive was his " History of British Birds," published in 1809. The best cuts in this volume were the tail pieces, which often displayed a love of country life and a whimsical or moralizing humour. The illustrations to " Aesop's Fables," published in 1809, were also often good ; but Bewick was, as an artist, by no means great ; his achievement is technical. That he was as a craftsman also well acquainted with the history of the craft is proved by the fact that he copied designs of Virgil Solis and other old woodcutters.

With Bewick's pupils and successors, such as Luke Clennell, Charlton Nesbit, William Harvey, Robert Branston, begins that form of xylographic activity which led eventually to the establishment of commercial houses, such as in England the Dalziels and Swains ; in Germany the Vogels, the Müllers, the Kretzschmars, the Ungers ; in France,

24

From Ugo da Carpi's Chiaroscuro print after Raphael's "Descent from the Cross." 14 × 11 in. [23]

From Frederick Sandys' Design : " The Old Chartist," cut by Swain. 1862. 4¼ × 5 in. [38]

C. Thompson's, who introduced the craft of engraving on the end grain into that country; further, the Pannemakers, the Pisans and Leloir Best; in America, W. J. Linton, Juengling, Johnson, and so forth. Mention should here also be made of George Baxter, whose patented colour process (1830), was founded on xylography.

It is usual to disregard these engravers, with the exception of George Baxter, whose productions are valued by a certain type of collector, and to speak only of the artists whose works they reproduced.

The slight on the craftsman which this disregard implies is hardly justifiable, seeing that only very few of the artists had any conception of the beauty and significance of the medium, and imposed upon the unfortunate wood engravers difficult, and often impossible, tasks.

Amongst the few who understood the medium, and whose designs deserve to be mentioned, though not quite in the same breath, with Dürer and Holbein, are Alfred Rethel, Ludwig Richter and Frederick Sandys; also occasionally Millais and Leighton. Rethel's two designs: " Death as a Friend " [36] and " Death the Strangler "; Richter's illustrations for Grimm's " Fairy Tales " and Frederick Sandys' " Old Chartist," [38] are worthy of their great prototypes.

This was, nevertheless, from the designer's point of view, " The Golden Decade " in English art, and in particular of illustration; and most of it was done in xylography. " No matter how little we like to acknowledge it," wrote Joseph Pennell in the first number of the Savoy, far back in 1896, " many of our luxuries and necessities come from Germany; and it is to Germany that one turns for the inspiration of modern illustration, and to Adolph Menzel [37] as its prophet."

Through Menzel's Prussian disciplining of his unfortunate wood-engravers, the xylographer was no doubt further spurred to efface himself; nor could he ever satisfy the artists in this respect.

This, however, is only natural and logical nemesis on a craft which from the Renaissance onward showed its tendency to sink its individuality, its true character, in that of other media, and so served its own aesthetic purposes only indirectly, and, as it were, by accident. The ideals which inspired this method of multiplication are somewhat pathetically revealed at its close by the Dalziels' " dying " confession: " When we look at the reproductions of tint drawings," they wrote at the beginning of this century,[1] " . . . . direct from the camera, we feel our occupation gone "; and then with a heroism amounting to self immolation: " In saying this we wish to add that we hail with

[1] " The Brothers Dalziel, a record of fifty years' work," London, 1901.

26

satisfaction the marvellous results from the many ingenious adaptations of photography and the consequent wide spread of the art of illustration." This is at once my excuse and my justification for refusing to pursue this note on the history of the craft any further, so far as " reproductions " are concerned.

The history of *creative* xylography begins where the Dalziels thought their occupation gone, and it is with xylography as a creative art that we are here concerned.

From " Robin Hood's Garland." XVII. Century.
[28]

Early XV. Century: German: " St. Christopher." 1423. After the
Print in the Rylands Library. [2c]

28

J. M. Papillon: "Headpiece." 1764. Original size. [29]

THE THIRD CHAPTER: DEALING WITH THE QUALITIES OF DESIGN AND CRAFT DURING THE PERIOD SURVEYED IN THE PRECEDING CHAPTER

IN seeking to appraise the value of xylography as a medium of design, rather than as means of multiplication, reproduction or interpretation, we must approach its development from another direction, *viz.*, that of the means employed by the *cutter* to gain his ends.

We notice then, first of all, that the early woodcuts at the commencement of the fifteenth century were substitutes for *pictures* rather than for drawings. The early woodcuts have a certain peculiarity of form, as indicated in their suave rounded and evenly thick outlines, which make it difficult to say whether they were actually cut in wood or in soft metal, and which causes them to look much like cartoons for stained glass.

The artist—if indeed he regarded himself as such—was mainly concerned with *clarity* of expression and with balance of composition. Clarity depended on an effort of his intellect, balance on the exercise of a natural sense, which even children and primitive races possess. The desire for clarity made him introduce only such figures or objects as were essential to his theme and, subject to the requirements of his sense of balance, in the order of their intellectual importance. The proportion of his figures, his mountains, his trees, would be regulated by the order of their subject value and not by their relation to optical truth. [2c] It is, however, misleading to speak of planes in this

29

connection, since to the primitive designer a picture was always a thing of a single plane, *viz.*, that of wall, panel or paper. It is this which gives the early wood prints a stability of composition and a clearness of statement which was subsequently lost.

So far then we have a design built of strong even contours, which latter were intended as the demarcation of the different colours applied to the print subsequently by hand. [2B] The method of obtaining the contour lines was the application of the knife and scorper to the plank of wood, but the change from the loop lines to the greater angularity and *woodiness* in the drapery of the second style [2A], after the first third of the fifteenth century, was not due to any aesthetic desire for the expression of the material; a similar change occurs likewise in the drapery of painted pictures, and was no doubt due to the introduction of a new kind of cloth.

In the woodcut this change is accompanied by the appearance of shading, produced by short parallel lines, which gives the design a greater plastic value, as we see in the block books. We may also notice here that the woodcutter by no means relied only on the knife for the purpose of producing his lines, which are often the result of a *pushed* tool, a scrive of some thickness. The block books are printed in a fine grey tone to leave the colourist a freer hand. Lettering occurs in the body of the cut and as part of the design. The unity of composition is in these books no longer so firm, but, nevertheless, in the best editions for example of the " Biblia pauperum," maintained by an architectural frame work. [5]

With the advent of the book printed with movable type the design becomes more palpably a drawing. But the earlier book illustrations are always designed with a view to colouring, and, therefore, mainly in outline. We may notice now that the cutter often leaves spaces of solid black, not necessarily as a value of light and shade, though in windows and door openings it has that appearance, but as a matter of colour. It was no doubt in its inception an economic device to save the labour of the colourist. Hatching and cross-hatching is resorted to, a feeble attempt at the latter [5B] may be seen in the Boccaccio's " De Claris Mulieribus," published in 1473, thirteen years earlier than the famous " Pilgrimage to Jerusalem," of Breydenbach. This latter book, illustrated by the Dutch painter Erhard Reuwich, of Utrecht, gives a particularly good example of the damaging influence the Renaissance had on aesthetic expression. It is illustrated by a great number of excellent cuts, in which the skilful use of the pushed tool,

30

From the Design by Alfred Rethel: "Death as a Friend." Cut by J. Jungtow. $12 \times 10\frac{3}{4}$ in.   [36]

31

From Petrus de Rosenhein's "Memorabiles Evangelistarum Figuræ."
Pforzheim. T. Anshelm. 1504. Original size. [4]

along with the drawn tool, is clearly evident. The text illustrations
have, in the best edition (1486), a virile, spontaneous character and an
aesthetically congruous style, testifying to the artist's keen appreciation of
actuality. [8] The much belauded title page on the other hand is loaded
with a veritable galaxy of Renaissance "star" performances. [7] The
page is crowded with a mass of scroll work. Saint Catherine occupies
the centre, flanked by two coats of arms under a sort of rose arbour,
in the branches of which a large number of naked children play hide
and seek. Were this cut, which in Johnson's book is hailed as "the

Early XV. Century: Block book: "Ars Memorandi." Page illustrating the Gospel of St. Matthew.
$4\frac{1}{2} \times 6\frac{7}{8}$ in.

[3]

From " Le Chevalier Délibéré," by O. de la Marche.   Holland :
Gouda, 1486.   7⅜ × 5 in.   [9]

finest engraving which had appeared up to that date," a metal engraving,
there might be some justification for the enthusiasm with which it is
commonly acclaimed, but even then it would need to be qualified;
it is stilted and confused, overcrowded and irrelevant, in short it has
rather more than the usual amount of vices that stultified the woodcut
as such—from the sixteenth century onward.
Only occasionally do we henceforward find work that maintains, or
indeed exceeds, the standard set by Reuwich's text illustrations. So
for example the wonderful illustrator of the Lubeck Bible (1494),
the illustrative qualities of which are remarkable for directness and

34

il cõprendre ne nõbrer tou
tes les diuerses formes et
manieres q to° les diuers
noms des peines isernales
Nõ michi si ligue centum sint
ozaqz centum/ferea vox omnes
sceleru cõpreheñdere forñs oña pe
ndrũ pezcurrere noía possī. Et
à ceste cause sõt elles bie a crai
ñdre et a doubter. Disoit doncqs
Lazarus ur assistens. Jay veu

en enfer premieremẽt sur
vne haulte mõtaigne tou
te ẽbrasée de feu z de sou
fre ardãt/grãde quãtite de
roes a moulins lesquelles tour
noient p grãt ĩpetuosite cõtinu
ellemẽt sans aucun repos. Et
aux parties exteriozes z interio
zes desdictes roez estoiẽt grãs
crãpons z ataches de fer ardãt
aufñlz estoiẽt pẽdues z atachees

õ ij

A page from " L'Art de bien vivre et de bien mourir " ; Paris : Antoine Vérard, 1492.   8¾ × 6⅜ in.   [14]

35

comparative simplicity; or the beautiful production of the Venetian Press: for example the elegant black line cuts of the " Malermi " Bible [10, 11] of 1490, with its dainty chapter headings subservient to the printed type, and manifestly designed by different cutters, not all of equal excellence; then the " Hypnerotomachia Poliphili," [12] published by Aldus, in 1499, remarkable not only for the simplicity of line, but the typographical taste and architectural structure. So also examples of the Florentine press, such as the " Giuochi di Scacchi," and the " Morgante Maggiore," of 1493 and 1500 respectively. Here, as everywhere in Florentine books, black is used with great decorative effect, both in the body and the borders of the cut, and the white line and plane employed with great effectiveness as *colour* values in borders and picture ornamentations.

The black line in these books of the turn of the century becomes more suave and more intricate, but also more shallow in France, where we can follow its development from " L'Art de bien vivre et de bien mourir," Paris, 1492 [14], to the attractive " Discours du Songe de Poliphile," of 1554, where the line is very refined, but despite greater realism in representation as characterless as drawn wire. [13]

One must, indeed, not imagine that earlier book production was guided by a very conscious aesthetic feeling: the aesthetic qualities came, if not always, at any rate, for the most part, haphazard.

So different, at the commencement of the Cinquecento, were the aesthetic sensibilities of the public—and it was the most *cultured* section of the public too—from our conceptions that the printers and publishers, such as Gruninger, Vérard and Wynkyn de Worde, did not hesitate to save trouble and expense in the following naïve manner: blocks of about three inches by one, representing figures, houses, trees or grass plots, were built up like a child's picture bricks into composite illustrations. Usually, five of such bricks were in this fashion united, surrounded by a black rule, and thus printed on one page of the text. The identical composite block might be repeated on the very next page; it might be used again in another part of the book. Then parts of it in combination with some different blocks would reappear in a different order and the same figures would represent different persons. Thus we find in editions of " Terence," both French and German, a figure representing " Geta " on one page becomes " Antipho " on another and " Parmeno " further on. More strangely still we find Wynkyn de Worde's (1510) edition of the morality play " Hycke Scorner " illustrated with single figures from Vérard's

36

¶ L'Accident

Autres si sõt a q̃ pour leurs richesses
En trauersãt quelque forest ou bois
Fais p brigãs faire grandes opresses
Q̃ tout leur ostent Voire z mainteffois
La Vie mesme par leurs cruelz explois.
Leur couppant la gorge/et mesmement
Font ces larrons et tout pareillement
A poures hommes cupdant que argent ayent
Plusieurs mourir en font a grant torment
Mais en fin dieu et iustice les payent

A page from " Les Loups Ravissans," published by Antoine Vérard, Paris, circa. 1500.
Original size.   [15]

"Terence" (1500), "Clitipho" [17] having become "Contemplacyon," "Chremes," "Pyte," and a figure sometimes called in "Terence," "Clinia," is reversed and represents now "Hycke Scorner" himself. Moreover, the admirable aesthetic unity between type and illustration—nowhere seen to greater advantage than in the "Malermi" Bible—which prevailed at first and, when it was undisturbed by hand colouring, was gradually destroyed with the increasing skill and naturalistic ambitions of the woodcutter and copper-plate engraver.

What, however, the Renaissance lost is ably pointed out by Paul Westheim, who prints a page from a "Rationarium Evangelistarum," of 1510 [4], side by side with a page of a block book, the "Ars Memorandi" of the beginning of the fifteenth century. [3] The subject in both cases is the "Quarta Mathei Imago." With the symbolism of the subject we are here not concerned: the more notice does the execution of the design deserve. The woodcutter of the later publication evidently intended to improve upon the earlier original (which looks as if it were a copy of a much earlier arch-type). He has indeed done his utmost to "call a spade a spade." Drawing, shading, perspective is much better, much "truer to life," but it has in course of this "improvement" lost every vestige of spiritual truth and aesthetic significance. No one could believe in this tow-headed doll and the asinine ass of the later "artist," certainly the artist himself did not, else he would not have had so much time for externals. Whether anyone could now believe in the earlier representation or not, it is manifest that its designer did; and because he believed, he treated every detail of the composition unhampered by actualities as part of a symbolically significant design within given limits. Note the feeble irrelevance of the border line in the later and the tectonic importance of the heavy border lines in the earlier print. Incidentally, the later print shows the encroachment of the cutter's or "formschneider's" activities on the colourists or brief-malers, the

From "Les Loups Ravissans." Antoine Vérard, Paris, 1492. 4 × 4½ in. [16]

38

Christoph de Jegher : " Hercules crushing Envy." Second quarter, XVII. Century.
$23\frac{1}{4} \times 13\frac{7}{8}$ in.   [26]

modelling and shading expressed in the wood lines naturally interfering with the colour.

That much of the aesthetic value of pure black and white which is manifest to us was not originally intended is made clear, for instance, by the following example. One of the best illustrated books published in Gouda, Holland, in 1486, is " Le Chevalier Délibéré " [9], by Olivier de la Marche, a *premier maître d'hôtel* to Emperor Maximilian. The cuts in this book are comparatively large, the handling remarkably free and *the black and white effect* of each composition particularly pleasing. Nevertheless, a record is preserved of the minute instructions as to composition and colouring given to the artist by the distinguished author for each single subject. For the one reproduced here the author prescibes[1]:

" The scene of this picture shall be a garden, in which there shall be put a little table with meat upon it, in the little wooden platter in the middle, and two glasses and a water-jug. And at this table shall be seated the author, dressed in a cloak of crimson satin, trimmed with small furs, and the said cloak shall be cut away over the sleeves, and the doublet shall be black, and on his head a hat with a golden image, and on his side there shall be written in a conspicuous place ' The Author.' And near by shall be seated the Hermit in his dress, and on his side he shall have written ' Understanding,' and they shall appear to be conversing together, and not far from them shall be a little novice to serve them in the costume above." Comparison with the cut shows how closely the illustration follows the prescription, and how little a " black and white " effect was contemplated.

With the advent of the sixteenth century the woodcut became of a set purpose more and more " calligraphic " and, as it were, ashamed of itself. To this rule there is at this early period only one exception. This is furnished by a remarkable artist who contributed some illustrations to a volume entitled " Les Loups Ravissans "—*fait et composé par maistre Robert Gobin, prestre maistre es ars.* . . . The volume was published about the year 1500. Three-quarters of it is taken up by a popular advice how " *cognoistre comment éviter vice et mal, on doit et tres vertueux estre.*" The " Loups Ravissants " are the devil as a wolf and his disciples, the Church being the shepherdess and her flock of sheep, the believers. The seventeen illustrations for the twelve chapters of this part of the book are dull and ordinary. The last quarter of the

[1]From " Le Chevalier Délibéré" by Olivier de la Marche. Preface by F. Lippman. The Monograph by the Bibliographical Society, No. 5.

Urs Graf: "Standard Bearer," beginning of XVI.
Century. $7\frac{1}{2} \times 4\frac{5}{16}$ in. [20]

book is a sort of " Totentanz," and describes *" Comment la mort de son pouvoir se vante, En accomplant le mal qu'aux humains fait."* The illustrations of this part, twenty-four in number, are of extraordinary interest: [15, 16] they are neither pictorial, in the sense of the primitive cut, nor calligraphic, in the sixteenth century sense, nor chalcographic, in the sense of the sixteenth and seventeenth century cuts which imitate line engraving. The figure of death is represented in accordance with the opening line of this part : *" Je suis la mort grande debellaresse"* as a woman-duellist or fighter-down, not as a skeleton ; the episodes are pictured with dramatic force. The cutting, however, is the most

K

41

remarkable feature ; for the cuts give the impression of having been *drawn* with the knife, *i.e.*, actually simultaneously with the cutting, so that the two operations seem one. It is manifestly all, or nearly all, knife work, though there is some evidence of the pushed tool also. The drawing is not faultless, but this defect is amply made up by the directness, the spontaneity of the cutting and the power and architectural sense of the design. It is true that the glyptic style of these cuts has a definite resemblance to blocks used by Antoine Vérard for the illustration of other books, such as the sumptuous " Thérence en François " (1515) [17], and the " Livres des Persécutions des Chrestiens " (1507), but none of these will compare in freedom, in composition and the handling of the knife, and in the use of black, with the " Grande debellaresse " cuts. In short, the " Grande debellaresse " illustrations are the first and for a long time only examples of the *creative* cut. What we admire in the more famous woodcuts, the works of Dürer and his contemporaries, followers and successors, is no longer the cutting of wood, but the design of the pen, and the skill of the cutter in preserving it. The aim of the artist becomes naturalistic with an increasing contempt for the natural limitations of tool and material. One may, I think, safely assume that if Dürer had continued to trouble about cutting wood himself, he would very soon have reformed the entire technique. Of all his work the " Apocalypse," it is said, is the one which he may have himself cut, and it is to be noted that very little cross-hatching appears in it, and even that is more feigned than actual : the effect being produced by chopping out little bits of wood rather than cutting with the knife round the contours of the "lozenges." It is to be noted too, that Dürer, as well as other designers of the period, this side of the Alps, makes little or no decorative use of solid blacks, and that the *white* lines, which frequently occur, are carefully disguised as black lines. An apparent exception is Urs Graf (1487 ? to 1530 ?), the Swiss goldsmith, die-cutter and engraver, whose figures of " Landsknechte " [20] and a " Family of Satyrs " are often quoted as early and good examples of white line cutting. They are drawn, unmistakably, in the metal chaser's white line manner, but in effect hardly more than reversed or negative black line drawings. Graf has put little thought into the use of his white lines, which have neither consistent light values nor any particular colour or decorative significance, though one of the " Landsknechte " with a white background is a much better example of white line cutting.

The division of labour, which relieved the creative artist of the trouble

42

"G.N.N." after Luca Cambiaso, middle of XVI. Century. $17\frac{3}{8} \times 12\frac{3}{16}$ in. [24]

that the cutting involved, and on the other hand stimulated the ambition of the craftsman to perform the difficult task of disguising the material and the tool, and making his designs resemble now a wash drawing (Ugo da Carpi) [23], now a pen line drawing (*e.g.*, Domenico Campagnola, Niccolo Boldrini after Titian, G.G.N. after Cambiaso), [24] now a copper engraving (*e.g.*, Virgil Solis, Koek van Alost, the Venetian engraver of Prescianesi, already mentioned, or numerous title pages, such as the Breydenbach one [7] and the one of Andreas Vesalius "de humani corporis fabrica," Basle, 1543), ultimately caused the decline of the woodcut, considered even as a craft only : it obviously could no longer compete with the kind of drawing which is germane to the graver and the metal plate. Interesting as some of the experiments had been, such as for example Domenico delle Greeche's (died 1580) gigantic free facsimile cut of Titian's " Death of Pharaoh," or Giuseppe Scolari's, who (likewise connected with the Titian school), [25] invented a forceful white line method of producing tonal effects, or many years later, Christoph de Jegher's (1627 or 1628 to 1652 or 1653) interpretative cuts after Rubens [26], they can, nevertheless, not be reckoned as works of *creative* art. This exception, that one must take to any work of art which is not executed in the material, or with the tools with which it was planned, will be better appreciated if we apply it to another branch of art, *viz.*, that of sculpture. A marble statue, when it is essentially a reproduction of a *clay* or wax model and done by other hands to boot, is exactly as far removed from creative art as a woodcut or engraving when it is essentially a reproduction of a drawing made *on* the wood. Works of creative art are in each case possible, *viz.*, in the first case, where the sculptor carves his own work directly out of the stone, or where the xylographer designs his cut with the tool. It is the gradual development of this standard of appraisement, this freeing of the tool and the material from alien fetters and restrictions which we have set ourselves to investigate. It is in this sense that the few, but remarkable, woodcuts of an etcher and painter of Rembrandt's school—Jan Lievens, must be mentioned. [27] Although, no doubt, the underlying drawings were done in pen and ink, Lievens has not allowed the pen line to do violence to the natural movement of the hand holding the scrive, the knife, the gouge. Moreover, the artist has made free use of the beautiful black, which the wood block yields, in a manner that pays due regard both to its colour and its light values.[1]

[1] Nevertheless it must be pointed out that at all events, in the case of the example here illustrated, there are in existence earlier *states* of the print with a far more conspicuous *woody* quality, proving that the artist intended to approach an etching-facsimile—in the *finished* state here shown.

44

Giuseppe Scolari: "St. George," end of the XVI. Century. $20\frac{7}{8} \times 14\frac{7}{16}$ in. [25]

By the end of the seventeenth century the craft, according to all authorities, had fallen into disrepute. It is of course true that as Chatto says[1] "At the period of the greatest decline of wood engraving, the want that was felt was not of working engravers to execute cuts, but of talented artists to design them." But when he points to the tail piece as an example of " wood engraving in its lowest state of declension," one cannot help noticing how immensely superior it is as a work of creative art, albeit unconsciously so, compared with the earlier and later specimens of wood engraving at its supposedly highest points. The cut is indeed crude, and the group of figures within the wreath —the principal characters in " Robin Hood's Garland," [28] *viz.*, "Robin Hood, Little John, Queen Catherine, the bishop, the curtal friar (not Tuck) and the beggar "—far from perfect, but the whole has clarity, decorativeness, and above all character, namely, that character which is born of simple statement and the frank use of the tool on its proper material.

In the eighteenth century J. M. Papillon's name stands highest, before Bewick, mainly because he imitated with remarkable skill copperplate engraving on wood. [29] He was the somewhat grandiloquent author of a treatise on the craft, by which he attempted to rescue it from what he necessarily regarded as its decline. But indeed, even the rough cut from a grocer's bill [32] here illustrated has not a little merit and when one compares the "refined " style and subject with a common cut from an English " broadside " used first for a " Horrid Deed " by S. Hodgson, of New Castle, in the year 1799 [33], one wonders whether the vulgar cut is not essentially a truer form of art than the refined cuts of the French engraver's manufacture. Cuts of the " Horrid Deed " kind were used in connection with executions generally, the features of the culprit being left black or indistinct, only the accompanying text being suitably varied. This cut, however, is of particular merit and shows Bewick's influence, if not hand, for it is an excellent example of his invention—the white line wood engraving.

Bewick's chief merit is that he starts from the wood block itself. [30] In all the work we had hitherto regarded the craftsman had started from the assumption that his problem consisted in carving his block so that it would imitate the black lines of a drawing. Bewick has nothing to do with the cutting of black lines at all: the black line with him—not at once: his early work is orthodox and negligible—was eventually, so to speak, the contour of the white line, and only in

[1]John Jackson—a Treatise on Wood Engraving—Historical portion by John Chatto.

46

Jan Lievens: "Portrait of a Cardinal." Middle of the XVII. Century. Original size. [27]

exceptional circumstances actually cut as a black line—for example, in dead branches of trees seen against a white sky. Moreover, Bewick worked with the graver on the end grain of (hard) box-wood. The nearest approach to his technique is Giuseppe Scolari's, [25] but Bewick, unlike Scolari, worked not only in white lines, but also in white *planes*, and correspondingly also in black planes. Furthermore, Bewick adopted an old practice of lowering the surface of the wood *before* engraving upon it, in all places which he wished to print lightly. By such means he was able to produce an effect of tone without having to rely only on the width and quantity of white (or black) lines, as the earlier woodcutters had to do. This *refinement* eventually ended in once more degrading the wood engraving to the status of an auxiliary craft, because the engravers were tempted to emulate the tonal qualities of paintings to the detriment of its structural or architectural stability and force. As a matter of fact, John Bewick, Thomas Bewick's brother seems—perhaps on account of his earlier death—to have saved his work from this particular danger, but drawn upon it Jackson's disapproval. " His (John's) style of engraving," said this authority, " is not good ; for though some of his cuts are extremely *effective* from the contrast of light and shade, yet the lines in almost every one are coarse and harsh, and ' laid in,' to use a technical expression, in a hard and tasteless manner." [31] Yet if one compares Jackson's reproduction of John Bewick's cut for " Poems by Goldsmith and Parnell " with its original, one is immediately struck with the latter's superior *glyptic* qualities as against Jackson's suave and sentimental, and characterless tooling.

The comparative ease with which the graver cuts on the end grain of hard wood is a temptation to the craftsman to refine his work more and more, and to evolve not only complicated systems of lines, but also other methods, such as dotting and " rotting " or worrying the surface of the wood, in order to express tonal, as against linear, qualities. There is, of course, no legitimate objection to this provided the engraver's aim remains within the scope of tools and materials. That, however, was precisely what the craftsman sought to overcome. Qualities necessitating the employment of a mass of, in themselves, meaningless lines were used in order to produce the effect of metal engravings, drawings, water-colour and oil paintings.

We had seen that the first complication of the craft was due to the artist designers who strove to give their forms an ever greater naturalistic and material character. The immediate result of this ideal

48

J. Johnson, del.   T. Bewick, sculp.

THE

HERMIT AT HIS MORNING DEVOTION.

Published January 1, 1804, by William Bulmer, at the Shakspeare Printing Office,
Cleveland Row.

From " Poems of Goldsmith and Parnell." Wood engraving by Thomas Bewick after
J. Johnson's design. 1804. Original size.   [30]

was the improvement in the quality of the drawing from the naturalistic point of view at the expense of clarity of expression. The conflict was due directly to the rival claims of the (supposedly absolute) *essence* and the (accidental) *appearance* of objects upon the consciousness of the artist. The second complication arose from the craftsman's desire to impart tone or colouristic qualities to his prints by other means than the hand, *i.e.*, by addition of a *tone* or colour block or blocks to the line block. The third complication arises from the craftsman's desire to make his block still less expressive of its own nature and to assume qualities which do not properly belong to it, *viz.*, that of copper, canvas, stone, etc.

So amongst Thomas Bewick's pupils and followers, particularly William Harvey, we find ingenious designs and results which vie successfully with copper-plate engravings in which the *white line* is applied with such finesse that its effect is that of the copper-plate engraver's black line. The nineteenth century School of Wood Engraving, resulted at least in part from these beginnings. The only artist at the beginning of the century, and indeed during its whole course until the nineties, who applied himself to creative cutting was, with the possible exception of one other—William Blake. We shall deal with this after having dealt with the methods of the reproductive or interpretative schools which flourished during that century.

Opposed to Bewick's *Tint* or *White* line school of engraving, the older Facsimile, or black line school, experienced a revival, though the cutting was done like Bewick's, on the end grain of hard wood. This revival was, as we have seen, due to one of the greatest draughtsmen of any country or age, Adolph Menzel, who more than any other artist inspired the generation of European illustrators that made the craft famous. Menzel employed French, English and German craftsmen, whose sole duty it was to cut his fine pen and ink lines in facsimile. But Menzel was a stern realist who drew from nature and not a calligraphist to whom the pen itself is a source of aesthetic inspiration [37]. There is not a single one amongst the marvellous range of his illustrations, his earliest and superficially calligraphic ones not excepted, in which one feels any emotion in the lines as such. For that very reason, his illustrations, wonderful as they are in all other respects, are yet never part of the printed page : they are insertions, interpolations in the text. Needless to say, they could, in such circumstances, not pretend to have any xylographic qualities. Menzel, indeed, did his utmost to force the xylographer into an attitude of slavish obedience.

50

John Bewick, del. et sculp.

THE SAD HISTORIAN.

Published January 1, 1804, by William Bulmer, at the
Shakspeare Printing Office, Cleveland Row.

From "Poems of Goldsmith and Parnell." Wood engraving
designed and engraved by John Bewick. Original size.   [31]

If, then, Menzel was " the inspiration of modern illustration," as Mr. Pennell contended, on the authority of " the artists and engravers and publishers themselves," it is not surprising that the productions of the craft as distinct from the original design from the thirties of last century to the commencement of the present one were aesthetically considered negligible.

This condemnation must not be misinterpreted. Regarded from the purely technical point of view, it is precisely the period of extraordinary achievement. Xylographers vied with each other not only in cutting " facsimile " with painstaking accuracy; they also applied all their ingenuity in order to render the most unlikely originals, watercolours, oil paintings, etchings, pencil and pen sketches, sculpture, textiles, ceramics, and at last photographs from nature faithfully and often convincingly in black and white.

Jonnard's interpretation of a Millet oil [40], Dalziel's rendering of a Birket Foster water-colour, [39] which we here illustrate, are worthy examples of wonderful technical achievement at different periods. The Facsimile cuts of the famous " sixties " were, if we accept the opinions of their designers, mostly *mutilations* of the drawings, the more so because apparently very few of the designers paid any attention to, or had any knowledge of, the problems which the xylographer had to overcome. It is more than likely that their very skill caused even Frederick Sandys, [38] Millais, Leighton, to give their engravers less xylographically suitable drawings than would have been the case if they had found themselves in Dürer's times.

It is interesting to note in this connection how Daumier drew his earlier illustrations with the manifest desire to simplify the wood engraver's task. His shading attempts to express form by the direction of the constituent parallel lines ; in his middle period the lines are free pen lines which the engraver only needed to cut in facsimile. In his third and last period, Daumier invests his drawings with that great massive weight which makes his art so memorable. The drawings are no longer done with the pen and the wood engraver has known how to render their individual quality with surprising success. To-day, however, the camera, as the Dalziels pointed out, does all this reproductive work with greater speed and greater accuracy.

As regards speed, the xylographer of last century not only made use of the camera for the purpose of transferring the design to the wood, he also practised a division of labour. The illustrations of topical events, published, *e.g.*, by the *Illustrated London News*, were done

52

From Adolph Menzel's Illustrations for Kugler's " History of Frederick the
Great " : " The Death of the King."   Cut by Unzelmann, 1842.   Original size.

[37]

From wood engraving by the Brothers Dalziel, after Birket Foster's picture "Cows in a Pool"; 1863. [39]

54

From a wood engraving by Jonnard after J. F. Millet's picture " La Tricoteuse "; 1889.　　[40]

on composite blocks, each part being handed to a different engraver, one of whom would perhaps do the clouds and sky, another the architecture, and a third the figures; or the division might be purely geometric, each doing a component square. It goes without saying that the rendering of textures by means of composite and specially devised tools was brought down to a formula, though to the end the best of the professional wood engravers deserve credit, and to be judged by the manner and the skill with which they applied themselves to this problem. There are engravings of butterfly wings, of armour, and Chinese vases which *qua* wood engravings are every bit as "artistic" and admirable as the famous etchings of a Jacquemart. And as to accuracy there is this to be observed that the hand can stress points which the eye sees, but which only the mind selects, a thing that can never be effected by means of the camera, which has no mind. It is not, therefore, from this point of view that xylography fails. It is when the professional xylographer attempts aesthetic achievements which are not based on creative design that he is doomed to failure, however great and admirable otherwise his skill.

A striking proof of this is furnished by the extremely accomplished and indeed marvellous technique employed by the American wood engraver Timothy Cole.

Cole belongs to the generation of artists who, steeped in the doctrines of impressionism, sacrificed everything to *tone*, with the result, in Cole's case, that his engravings seem to render not so much the originals he reproduces as the effect of soft and silvery platinotypes with photographic accuracy. A Duccio di Buoninsegna [41, 41A] and a Vermeer van Delft, thus rendered in black and white, by a black which is not black and a white which is not white, look as if they had been contemporaries and compatriots of Whistler.

A translation of a painting into the technique of xylography is both possible and aesthetically justifiable, but the problem should be approached from an entirely different angle.[1]

Reproductive engravings, whether they be of Cole's or of Linton's school may be compared with the orchestra imitations on mechanical "players"; whilst the aesthetically permissible translation of one medium into another is analogous to the translation of an orchestra into a piano-score.

In other circumstances wood engraving, however accomplished, is less

[1] Professor E. Wurttemberger's "Zeichnung, Holzschnitt und Illustration," Basel, 1919, should be studied in this connection.

56

From Timothy Cole's wood engraving, after Duccio, in the Duomo, Siena. 1892. [41]

Enlarged portion of Timothy Cole's wood engraving of Duccio's
Painting.   [41A]

accurate than photography and aesthetically less justifiable than a J. R.
Smith mezzotint, a George Wille line engraving, or a Charles Waltner
etching, in each of which the technique employed makes the most,
not the least, of the material.

The aesthetic objection to all *reproductive* engraving is, however,
based on the divorce of the original design from the method and
character of the material and the tools with which the engraving is
produced. The wood engraver has to employ a score of tool marks
to render the " quality " of a single stroke of the brush. If he succeeds
in this to an appreciable extent it is a proof of marvellous craftsmanship, but has no relation whatever to creative art, which latter is always
a question of *original* design.

M   57

For such reasons one will to-day acknowledge the skill of Urushibara, the Japanese, who manages to produce an almost exact facsimile of a Brangwyn water-colour [64] by means of no less than fifty separate printings, just as one will admire Bangemann's facsimile renderings in xylography of Liebermann's pen and ink drawings; or Kruger's colour engravings of the old masters.

But none of these achievements must blind us to the fact that they are not creative art.

And even when the original design is the craftsman's own, as is the case with some of Urushibara's, and many other modern colour prints based on the Japanese method, creation suffers in course of its sublimation, because the mind is divided against itself—creation and execution become two consciously separate processes.

From a " Broadside," by Bewick (?) " Horrid Deed." A.D. 1799. Original size.

[33]

58

From "Ten Spiritual Designs," by Edward Calvert. The wood engraving: "Christian Ploughing the Last Furrow of Life." 1829. Original size. [35]

THE FOURTH CHAPTER: CREATIVE DESIGN IN XYLOGRAPHY: ITS ORIGIN AND FIRST DEVELOPMENTS

GRANTED that the illustrators of the Victorian era, the Keenes and Sandys, the Dorés and Millais and Rossettis, the Boyd Houghtons, Du Mauriers and Birket Fosters *è tutti quanti*, were great and some-times prolific designers for wood engraving, it is no use disguising the fact that their activity contributed nothing to the *art* of xylography, which they treated as a purely ancillary craft and scolded as a cinderella ugly-sister-wise. Even the best of them, with the exception perhaps of Charles Keene, paid little enough attention to truly xylographic design and none of them any to its glyptic qualities and possibilities. Not a black that was not wantonly broken, barely a grey that was not produced by cross-hatching, and hardly a white that was not marred by a "tint" or a meandering scribble. Had any of these artists ever had to engrave their own designs they would have quickly reformed the craft and themselves to boot.

59

But designing was regarded as art and, therefore, a genteel occupation; engraving was a tradesman's business. The only wonder is that the poor engravers did not lose their minds as well as their eyesight more frequently. The continuance of this, for Europeans, nefarious practice of division of labour as between artist and craftsman is the more remarkable because at least one great artist had, at the beginning of the nineteenth century, shown a better way : William Blake.

The idea came to William Blake as the result of a spiritual revelation : the voice of his dead brother Robert gave him the full recipe for the production of his " Songs of Innocence " by a metal process which enabled him to print both text and illustrations simultaneously from an acid-bitten copper-plate.

Here was, indeed, the unity not only of design and execution, but also of the two with the text, such as it existed in the old block books, once more established; and the affinity was greater than might appear, because Blake's metal process was a *relief* process like the woodcut. Here, then, we have a truly ideal combination : poet and painter, printer and " cutter " were one and the same person. It is this desire for unity in design and execution no doubt which made him later (in 1821), when he was commissioned by Dr. Thornton to illustrate an edition of Ambrose Phillips' " Imitation of Virgil's First Eclogue " with wood engravings [34], decide to cut his designs himself, with the sequel that their publisher thought it advisable to apologize for result thus obtained in the following manner :

" The illustrations of this English pastoral are by the famous Blake, the illustrator of Young's " Night Thoughts " and Blair's " Grave," who designed and engraved them himself. This is mentioned as they display less of art than genius, and are much admired by some eminent painters."

To-day we may smile at this somewhat apologetic recommendation, but we can understand it, and even appreciate its entire relevance and necessity. What the publisher here calls art is what we of to-day would call craftsmanship, or technique; what he calls genius is something he manifestly did not himself comprehend, but the presence of which he vouched for on the authority of " some eminent painters."

Technically, that is to say : judged by the standard of Papillon, or even of Bewick, not to mention Dalziel or Cole, Blake's cutting is negligible and, indeed, of childlike innocence: " They are done," said Edward Calvert, " as if by a child, several of them careless and incorrect, yet there is a spirit in them humble enough and of force

Two of William Blake's woodcuts for Ambrose Phillips'
"Imitation of Virgil's First Eclogue." Original size. [34]

enough to move simple souls to tears." How then is this *genius* cognizable? Comparison with contemporary work will make it clear that Blake's cuts, whether "careless and incorrect" or not, are of the utmost simplicity. They are almost entirely white line cuts and show their connection with the block of wood without shame.

Therein lies the affinity of Blake's with the craftsmanship of the early woodcutters. He, like they, had something to express, cared not for "art" as such, and did not, therefore, trouble to disguise the tool or the material. With him the "wheel had come full circle." Blake arrives at the end of one great revolution of the wheel of life, and at the same time at the commencement of another.

Edward Calvert, a pupil of Blake's, is the link that connects the latter with the older generation of those living artists who, following consciously or unconsciously in Blake's footsteps, have revived the craft in the creative sense. Calvert died as late as 1883—his work little known and forgotten, until its exhibition arranged at the British Museum, in 1891, by Sir Sidney Colvin.

The difference between Calvert's attitude towards his art, and on the one hand Blake's, on the other Bewick's, is one of mental constitution. Blake, as his publishers truly said, was a genius—Bewick a craftsman —Calvert a representative of talent. Blake's, as the creative artist's, consciousness of his work is related solely to that which he is urged to express by it from an inner necessity ; Bewick's, as the craftsman's consciousness is related mainly, if not entirely, to the manner of expression. In Jackson's book one comes across a sentence which is illuminating in this respect, though it does not refer to Bewick, but to Branston. " Mr. Branston, like many others, did not think highly of the cuts in Bewick's fables ; and feeling persuaded that he could produce something better *he employed* Mr. Thurston *to make several designs* with the intention of publishing a similar work."

Here, then, we have the *craftsman*, employing the *artist* whose design is regarded mainly as a means for the display of craftsmanship. This attitude of mind is a common one from which the "schools" in art result. The consciousness of minds like Calvert's, partakes of the nature of both artist and craftsman, and approaches, according to the strength of the creative or the assimilative urge, more to genius or to handicraft as the case may be.

Calvert, a cultured man (which Blake was not, in the ordinary sense of the word), is a minor lyrical poet turned artist. Consciously affected by Blake, yet conscious likewise of Bewick's craftsmanship, his work

62

Felix Vallotton : " Portrait of Robert Schumann." [43]

63

holds a position between the two. He produced a series of " Ten Spiritual Designs," of which six were on wood, two on copper and two on stone ; yet the actual method of his drawing is almost identical. His imagination is tender, romantic, refined and charming. Of his "Christian Ploughing the Last Furrow of Life," [35] George Richmond spoke as a work of great beauty in the prints, but as drawn upon the block before it was cut, of superlative beauty. We have then here, so to speak, " Bewick " trying to become " Blake " through the person of Calvert, in the same way as we had " Thurston " called upon to outdo " Bewick " in the person of Branston. Calvert rather than Blake foreshadows the change of the artist's consciousness which is responsible for the subsequent development of xylography.

That movement which took place at the beginning of the eighteen-nineties, and which is generally spoken of as a revival of the craft, is, in point of fact, a re-birth, seeing that its germination is due to a new spirit. The modern woodcut, dating from that period, is not in essence the fruit of public demand, like the early single woodcuts of the fifteenth century, nor of economic necessity, such as the later book illustrations of the same and the sixteenth centuries, and is not really even a method of multiplying designs, which by " the Nineties " the photographic camera was better able to do. The *raison d'être* of the modern woodcut is due to the free choice of artists drawn to the craft partly by considerations which, however associated, are fundamentally aesthetic ; partly by the *physical* attraction which the material and the tools of a craft exercise, in any period on every fine craftsman.

The generation which began this re-creation of the woodcut is the older generation of living artists, many of whom are still practising this medium of artistic expression. Moreover, the influences which have modified the design are not to be sought only in the development of the craft. They lie to a great extent outside. A mere chronological account of the output during the last thirty years or so would, therefore, hardly explain the extraordinary differences which are manifest in the conception and execution of modern xylographic design, differences which are greater than any previously experienced within a much larger space of time. It would seem preferable to investigate the main influences which have determined the changes in the outlook of the artists who have made the woodcut deliberately a means of artistic expression.

Bewick's principal achievement was the establishment of the black plane as the basis of his design, which was cut out of this plane by

Felix Vallotton : " L'Averse," from J. Meier-Graefe's " Felix Vallotton." [44]

HERO AND LEANDER ❧ BY
CHRISTOPHER MARLOWE
AND
GEORGE CHAPMAN

❧Hero's description and her love's;
The fane of Venus where he moves
His worthy love-suit, and attains;
Whose bliss the wrath of Fates restrains
For Cupid's grace to Mercury:
Which tale the author doth imply.

From Charles Ricketts' opening page for Marlowe and Chapman's "Hero and Leander." 1894. Original size.　　　　[45]

THE TREE
OF KNOWLEDGE.

ROM what
meek jewel
seed
Did this
tree spring!
How first beat its new life
in bleak abode
Of virgin rock, strange met-
als for its food,
Towards its last hewn
mould, the bitter rood!
First did it sprout, indeed,
A double wing.

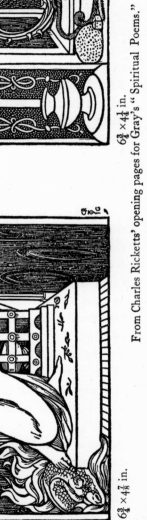

6¾ × 4¼ in.

From Charles Ricketts' opening pages for Gray's "Spiritual Poems."

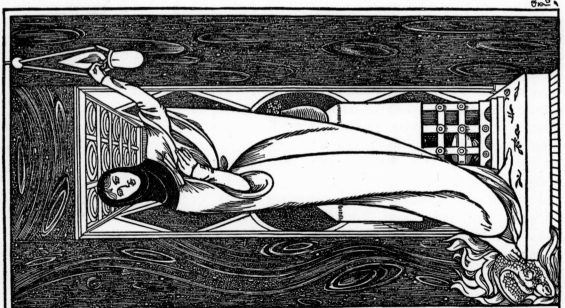

6¾ × 4⁷⁄₄₈ in.

[46]

67

means of a system of white lines; but his particular significance lies in the fact that his *lines* were not all lines in the draughtsman's sense of the word, but very frequently white and black *planes*—though not quite in the painter's sense of light and shade. Herein lies a basic affinity of the white line cut with impressionistic painting, which also works in planes from the darks upward to the light, by gradual elimination of the dark surface, in contradistinction to drawing generally and the etcher's drawing in particular, which is virtually a gradual elimination of the white surface. There is also an affinity of this method of design with wood or stone carving—that is to say, a freeing of the " design " from the material by a series of gradual eliminations. This peculiarity of the white line design has the beneficial tendency of stabilizing the composition which can develop only by subtraction inwards, whereas the black line design has the tendency to grow beyond control by addition outward and, therefore, to leave things too much at the mercy of sudden " inspirations." The relevance of this observation will become clearer presently; for the moment we will only note that the white line approach to the wood block design is essentially pictorial, whilst the black line approach is purely graphic.[1] We may, therefore, expect to find, as we actually do, two different developments in xylographic design—one which has the pictorial plane, the other which has the graphic or calligraphic line as its basis. In 1887, Manzana Pissarro, a son of Camille's, had decorated the catalogue of his father's exhibition with a " Peacock " design, cut directly in wood with white line excisions. This experiment he followed up, some three or four years later, with a " Turkey " for a catalogue of his own exhibition. These designs are virtually flat wood carvings printed upon paper, and without a brush or a pencil foundation. He may thus probably claim to be regarded as the first of the moderns to have used tool and material in this way—but his achievement was hardly acknowledged.

The year 1891, that had introduced Calvert to the British public, through the exhibition of his prints at the British Museum, informed the French of a newly risen woodcutter, Felix Vallotton, a Swiss, living in Paris, who was then commencing a long activity with a series of woodcuts, beginning with a portrait of Verlaine, in a curiously novel, but uncertain, technique. Verlaine's portrait was made up of a series of black lines, which, however, seem to have been produced by white line cutting. The superficial effect of the portrait is not unlike a wood

---

[1] I use the word in its original and truer sense, because there is no better to take its place.

68

From Lucien Pissarro's " The Queen of the Fishes " :
" Les Bûcherons." 2 × 3½ in.   [50]

engraving, in the reproductive sense, the general effect is decidedly
pictorial. Two years later (1893), we have an excellent likeness of
Schumann cut white out of the black ground—the effect is entirely
pictorial and only close observation of its details shows that its basis
is graphic, [43] but it is the kind of drawing directly due to the impressionist theories of the period. It is only the artist's reluctance to allow
the dark hair of the composer to merge into the equally dark background without a line of demarcation which proves him to have been
uncertain in the logic of his design.

The same year in which, along with other interesting cuts of Vallotton's,
this Schumann portrait appeared, two young artists in England
commenced a long series of woodcut illustrations which showed the
revival of the black line cut, based on delicate pen design—I refer to
Charles Ricketts and Charles Shannon, who, as the result of eleven
months' collaboration, produced their first woodcut book " Daphnis and
Chloe." This was illustrated with thirty-seven cuts, of which fifteen
were designed by Charles Shannon, whilst the actual cutting was done
by the two artists working mutually on each other's blocks. Both
artists were trained as wood engravers of the old school and, therefore,
well acquainted with the white line, but this book, as well as their
next one, the "Hero and Leander," of 1894, [45] was deliberately
evolved from the " Hypnerotomachia di Poliphilo," not only in the
black line method of design, but in the typographical aspect generally.
As book builders, and, indeed, in the quality of the designs, as well
as the cutting, the two English artists show themselves both technically

69

From Lucien Pissarro's illustration for Flaubert's " St. Julien
L'Hospitallier." Published by the Eragny Press. 3½×3½ in.
[51]

and aesthetically superior to their predecessors. The books subsequently issued by their " Vale Press," for which Ricketts not only
designed three fonts of type, but also invented and cut in wood
nearly all the borders, frontispieces, most of the illustrations, as well as
end papers, cover papers and bindings, ushered in a new era of book
building generally. Amongst this artist's principal woodcut illustrations the following should be mentioned : Six circular cuts for the
English, and a little later, five cuts for the Latin Edition of Apuleius'
" Cupid and Psyche,"; frontispieces, borders and initials for William
Blake's " Book of Thel " and " Poetical Sketches "; the same for
Milton's " Early Poems," Drayton's " Nymphidia and Muses
Elyzium," Gray's " Spiritual Poems " [46], and lastly ten woodcuts
for " The Parables of the Gospels," these in a freer and more
personal style of black line cutting.
The ideals and ideas which guided the creator of these book produc-
tions have been adequately explained by Ricketts in his " Defence
of the Revival of Printing."
Ricketts and Shannon had started an aesthetic magazine, " The Dial,"

70

SONGS BY BEN JONSON.. A SELECTION FROM THE PLAYS, MASQUES, AND POEMS, WITH THE EARLIEST KNOWN SETTINGS OF CERTAIN NUMBERS.

THE ERAGNY PRESS, THE BROOK, HAMMERSMITH, LONDON, W.

From a Title-page for "Songs by Ben Jonson," produced by Lucien Pissarro. Slightly reduced.   [49]

From Auguste Lepère's woodcut " Les Bûcherons." $8\frac{3}{8} \times 5\frac{3}{4}$ in. [53]

in 1889, and this magazine contained not only numbers of original woodcuts, by other artists, but also xylographic reproductions of pen designs by Ricketts and Reginald Savage. One is in particular characteristic of the whole outlook of this " school " ; it is called ' Centaurs,' " an experiment in line designed by Reginald Savage, drawn and engraved on the wood by Charles S. Ricketts." It appeared in the third number of " The Dial " in 1893. It is hardly a good line drawing and it is difficult to see what was gained by cutting it in wood, since as a method of reproduction this was no longer necessary ;¹ but its ingenious variations on a single theme—scilicet the black line —not the accidental subject matter " the Centaur " (an " animal " which, incidentally, haunted the imagination of many artists of his period), are interesting as pointing to the radical difference between the primitive designer's and the nineteenth century artist's mind. For this is the period of the pen line design, which commenced with Menzel and ended with Aubrey Beardsley, in whose sensitive hand the linear texture of design was changed from Menzel's solid web of facts to an airy filigree of fancy. The subject interest from this angle of vision is entirely merged into, if not indeed ousted by, the interest in the treatment.

Beardsley's arrangement of black and white had an enormous international influence on illustration generally, and the massed black was particularly attractive to the artists who felt themselves drawn to the woodcut.

Whether Vallotton's subsequent evolution, in which he makes, increasingly, use of black masses is owing to Beardsley, I do not know, but the fact is that he employs it with dramatic intensity for the heightening of effect in subjects of Zolaesque realism, imparting to them not only a realistic and dramatic appeal, but also a purely aesthetic one. Compare, e.g., " La Manifestation," " L'Exécution," "Le Suicide," " L'Averse " [44] with "L'Absoute" and "La Paresse." The dramatic and ephemeral, in subject, is thus wedded to the aesthetic and permanent in treatment.

We now come to another aspect of the woodcut of this period, in which France and England appear once more linked. In the pages of " The Dial " there are reproduced nine cuts by Lucien Pissarro. Pissarro, as a son of one of the great impressionist painters, strikes a somewhat incongruous note in that particular " galère." The polite

¹Mr. Savage has explained to me that the idea was in some way to give the effect of " chiaroscuro " without having recourse to a second block.   I confess I do not understand this.

From T. Sturge Moore's woodcut illustrations for Guerin's
"Centaur—The Centaurs' Wedding." Original size. [55]

ingratiating suavity which characterizes the line of the English artists
is replaced by one of robust and rustic simplicity in Pissarro's woodcuts
of Peasants [50] or country girls (Solitude, Ruth, Orpah and Naomi,
Ruth the Gleaner). The black line is no longer calligraphic, but purely
utilitarian as in a painter's sketch; that is to say, it helps to give a
three-dimensional illusion to the two-dimensional plane of the print.
On the other hand, a cut such as "Le petit chaperon rouge" or the
white deer from "St. Julien L'Hospitallier" [51] is calligraphic and
English enough to have had Walter Crane for its designer, though the
cutting—a mixture of black and white line—gives it a quality which
Crane, who did not cut, did not employ. Lucien Pissarro was driven
from France by his admiration for the style of Charles Keene, one of
the few English artists of the time who himself understood the craft
for which his designs were made. But Keene's manner was not at
all to the liking of the French taste—the Impressionists excepted, and
so Lucien sought refuge in this country where he established his own,
i.e., the "Eragny" Press. Lucien's aims differed from those of the
Vale press mainly in the combination of a fuller colour scale with the
text and illustrations [49]. The French artist, trained in the school of
his father's impressionism, soon hit upon the idea of mixing white
with his printing colours so that the printed book page preserved an
evenness of tone values upon which the impressionist painters laid
much emphasis. Lucien's colour-interpretations of his father's designs

o

in " La Charrue d'Erable " represent extraordinary feats of economy in means and fullness in effect, whilst the beautiful " Livre de Jade " and " L'Histoire de Soliman-Ben Daoud...," and particularly the opening pages of the latter, are, as examples of typographical illumination, unsurpassed.

Another metamorphosis of Impressionism is represented by Auguste Lepère's xylography.

Lepère started as a wood engraver of the old school and as such achieved some remarkable feats of tone and texture engraving, as for example in his " L'abbreuvoir à l'île St. Louis " [52] or his " Sortie du Théâtre du Châtelet." When, however, he took up woodcutting with the knife, he produced black and white and colour prints in which pen and brush drawing is reproduced with remarkable fidelity. " Le coupeur des bouts de cigars," " Le Paysagiste " or " La Fin de Journée " in which the same applies to a tinted pen drawing. None of Lepère's work has, however, real glyptic qualities [53]; the design is wholly independent of the material, and regarded purely as designs they are often lacking in balance and concentration. He was happier and more consistent in his etching.

We return once more to " The Dial " because it contains also the work of an artist who has developed the Calvert tradition of engraving in a modern sense: T. Sturge Moore. Both as a poet and as an engraver of wood this artist treads his own secluded paths. True, there are amongst his woodcut designs like " The Death of the Dragon," which show him in sympathy with Ricketts' and Savage's " experiments in line "; others again like the treatment of the " Unicorn Press " device show his interest in the early Italian manner. Sturge Moore's conception of art and its function in life is exalted, his technique far from facile, his drawing even not always good. His wood engravings, wrought with much glyptic subtlety, therefore do not yield their full charm or significance at the first glance; when once, however, the mind has attuned itself to Moore's xylographic language, it will enjoy his variations of mood from the religious (" Go wash ") to the humorous (" Centaurs conversing " and " Centaurs' Wedding " [55]), from the classic (" Pan as an Island " [54]) to the Wordsworthian worship of nature, and the imagination displayed in his book plates.

The pictorial rather than the purely graphic vision characterizes the work of an English artist who has had a considerable influence, less perhaps on the woodcut than on the evolution of design in general:

74

From Auguste Lepère's wood engraving: " L'Abbreuvoir à l'île de St. Louis."
$12 \times 15\frac{7}{8}$ in.   [52]

From T. Sturge Moore's woodcut : " Pan as an Island." 7½ × 5 in. [54]

William Nicholson. His series of Twelve Portraits, amongst which a capital likeness of Queen Victoria, just verging on caricature, created quite a popular stir, so general was the appreciation of the novelty as which the "woodcut" was regarded. This appreciation was maintained for his "Almanac of Twelve Sports," his "Alphabet," his "London Types," and led, in 1902, to another series of twelve portraits, amongst which the sly and "slim" looking Li-Hung Chang, of "Boxer" fame, is an extraordinary bit of shrewd observation, and "Sada Yacco," the Japanese actress, [56] by reason of the ingenious bamboo screen background, a particularly good example of design. These woodcuts, though several of them appeared in book form and with a specially heavy form of type, were indeed principally decorations. Their pictorial unity was further enhanced by a second (lithographic) buff-coloured tone and by touches of other positive colours, applied either by hand or by lithography. Curiously enough the treatment sometimes, and in spite of all embellishments, tended towards the photographic, owing to a difficulty with which every wood designer has had to contend, ever since the Renaissance began to set store by representational accuracy: the manipulation of the black, which in part does duty as a colour value, is in part also a light value. Nicholson's bold black masses represent a compromise, and as a general rule an exceptionally happy one; it is only occasionally that the black when it is, too frankly, a light-value, lends the composition a photographic appearance. Nevertheless, regarded as individual and independent works, [57] and contributions to the art of decoration and the graphic arts in general, his prints occupy a place in the front rank. The original source of Nicholson's xylographic inspiration, it should be noted, is to be found in the elder Crawhall's whimsical "forgeries" of old chapbooks with which he delighted the literary world in the early eighties. Such things as "Old ffrendes wyth new faces," or "Chapbook Chaplets," owe their whole conception to delightful but purely literary and associative ideas; aesthetic considerations entered hardly, if at all.

Drawing their original inspiration from these same sources, Gordon Craig's woodcuts, and typography too, display more carefully-considered aesthetic intentions than their prototype. Gordon Craig is the "father-in-aesthetics" of Lovat Fraser, whose famous "Polly" seems to have walked on to the "Lyric" stage, straight from Crawhall's chapbook "A True Relation of Mrs. Veal to Mrs. Bargrave." I mention this here apparently irrelevant fact (Lovat Fraser did not

From William Nicholson's hand-coloured proof of the Portrait of Sada Yacco. $9\frac{3}{8} \times 9\frac{3}{4}$ in. [56]

From William Nicholson's Portrait of Andrew Ainslie Common, Esq., F.R.S., LL.D.   10×9½ in.   [57]

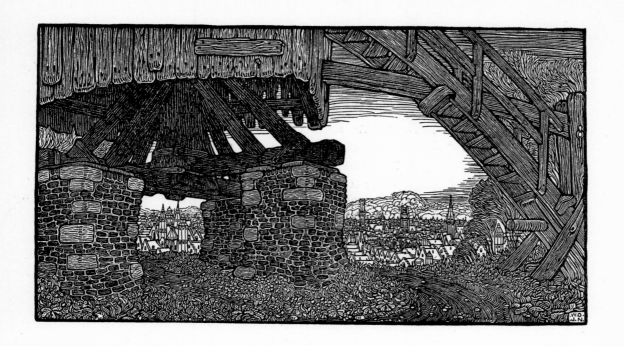

From W. O. J. Nieuwenkamp's woodcut: "Mill at Bruges." $8\frac{1}{4} \times 15\frac{7}{8}$ in.

cut his type ornaments and book illustrations in wood), because it helps our orientation. Craig's art, like his disciple's, is not only theatrical in virtue of its immediate association—compare his four cuts for Hugo von Hofmannsthal's "Der Weisse Faecher"—but in its entire complexion. Craig's ideal is neither the essence of things, their abstract and permanent idea (as the Greeks endeavoured to see it), nor even the appearance of things as modified by the transient factors of accident (as the Impressionists endeavoured to see them); his is a world of feigned actuality—like the actor's. It is presumably this fact which makes his woodcutting so intensely interesting. He does not translate drawings into wood ; he is not hampered by classic, gothic, renaissance or realistic and romantic ideals of art—or technique. As a consequence he is the first to use the xylographic tools in order to " stage " xylographic effects. One will find in his technique all imaginable variations of cutting : black line, white line, black and white masses, dotted texture, combinations of grey tones produced by the breaking of black lines with white lines, so that one gets the effect almost of two printings (compare " d'Artagnan's Man " in the second volume of his magazine "The Page," 1899). All the devices which the commercial tone engraver used are, as it were, extracted, enlarged and promoted from the insignificant rôles of tonal servants to the principal actors in his designs. Craig has cut hundreds of blocks, and it is characteristic of him that he bestows equal care on small detail of theatrical properties (compare the cutting of the design for a headdress in the same number of " The Page ") as on the most important ones (compare the " Rainbow " from the Weisse Faecher). In addition to experimenting with the manner of cutting, Craig has invoked the aid of heavy type, coarse and tinted paper, together with touches of positive colour applied by hand. There is no greater contrast imaginable than that of William Blake's and Gordon Craig's outlook and yet there is something of the child in each. Their work is not serious in Bewick's or in Lepère's sense ; hence both puzzled their contemporaries, Blake's publisher excusing his childlikeness with a lack of art ; and the " Studio Magazine," of the day, opining that the cuts of " The Page " " by the naïveté of their technique disarm criticism." But there is this fundamental similarity between them; both believe: Blake in the reality of his figments, Craig in the fictitiousness of his realities.[1]

---

[1] Owing to the Artist's objection to the faithfulness of the line block and the Writer's objection to the unfaithfulness of the half-tone process, the illustrations of Craig's works have had to be omitted.

78

From Sydney Lee's woodcut: "The Ravine."   30 × 22 in.

Before bringing this survey of the Pioneer era to a close let us briefly survey once more the position the woodcut had reached in England at about this time. In December, 1898, "The first exhibition of original wood engraving " was held in this country, *viz.*, at the Dutch Gallery, in Brook Street. The contributors included mainly the contributors to "The Dial," Ricketts, Ch. Shannon, Moore, Savage, Lucien Pissarro, and—as the only outsiders—Nicholson and Jean François Millet; the contribution of the latter being in all probability one of the only five out of eight that were engraved as well as designed by him, in a style of pen-drawing. The period then marks a definite stage in the development of the woodcut. The designation " original wood engraving," by which the contributors to this exhibition sought to distinguish their work from other specimens of xylography, plainly shows that the artists were anxious to establish a clear-cut distinction between the wood engraving of the common press and their own. What is not so clear, however, is their view of the nature of this difference. Ricketts and Shannon, we had seen, drew their own designs on the wood and engraved them in facsimile. On the other hand, Ricketts engraved a design of other artists, Legros' and Savage's to wit. Incidentally, we may mention here that amongst all the engravings of his unusually accomplished pen designs, and he executed at that time a great many illustrations for the Essex House Press, Savage's " Behemoth," which appeared in " The Dial," is undoubtedly the best, both as a pen design and as a reproduction of wood engraving. The question then is whether the fact that an artist engraves *his own* design is of sufficient importance to establish the resulting wood print as an " original " engraving: as for example in the more recent, but manifestly Ricketts-inspired typographical decorations designed by F. W. Sargant. Might not an author's manuscript with equal justification be regarded as an " original " production ? Quite as misleading is the word " original " in connection with wood engraving, unless the engraving modifies the original design in vital respects : a mere "stiffening" of lines, however, would not constitute a vital modification. In examining the work of the artists so far mentioned, with the possible exception of Sturge Moore, we notice several degrees of modification. Ricketts', Shannon's and Savage's admitted very little. It is true, of course, that Ricketts in some of his engravings, for instance in his title page for " The Spiritual Poems of Gray," [46] introduced some decorative white line engraving which could only conveniently be designed *in* and not *on* wood ; nevertheless, on the whole

80

From a woodcut by Sydney Lee: "The Cottage Doorway." 6¾×7¼ in.   [60]

the cutting is " facsimile " even though the artist changed the design
in details on the wood as the cutting progressed. If there is any point
in deciding the priority of a really *original* cut a little landscape tail
piece in white line by H. P. Horne, printed in the " Century Guild
Hobby Horse," of 1883, is an earlier and truer form of *original* wood
engraving than any. It has, so far as I can see, no aesthetic ancestors,
no historical pedigree, it does not imitate, develop or improve upon
any earlier method and it is difficult to see what other medium could
have originated it. Otherwise, however, it is of very little value or
importance.

P   **81**

No, the immediate reasons for the English revival were purely associative. If Ricketts and his group improved and developed the Italian manner of woodcutting, Morris and his assistants Hooper, Sleigh, Gaskin, Gere, were inspired by the Germanic style, Burne Jones forming a " Keltic " link between the former aristocratic and the latter guild-democratic camps. Even such a remarkably large-sized cut as William Strang's " Plough "—it measured 5 ft. by 6 ft. and was composed of nine blocks 24 in. by 20 in.—was, if not in dimensions, certainly in design, Holbein-inspired, and the artist is said to have had some assistance from Robert Bryden in the cutting. Strang's " Doings of Death," a series of Chiaroscuro prints, were cut partly by Sleigh and partly by Bryden. The latter xylographer, however, deserves recognition as the author of a series of woodcut portraits published by Dents, in 1899. They represented the literary giants of the period, *e.g.*, Tennyson and Browning, Stevenson, Tolstoy and Ibsen. They were, in their time, brave and bold experiments in frank cutting, but seem, compared with later work, restrained and slightly disguised translations of photographs into xylography.

Originality was then, in any true sense, hardly the main characteristic of any of these artists. Much more truly " original " was the work of two other pioneers of the period, one of them English, the other Dutch : Sydney Lee and W. O. J. Nieuwenkamp.

W. O. J. Nieuwenkamp's views of his native country [58] are, if, as he says, inspired by Dürer, yet done in a peculiar linear technique entirely his own, which, however, in such prints as his " Wave," show a distinctly Japanese source of inspiration. Attracted to the craft by the interest aroused in the Japanese woodcut, mainly owing to the Goncourts' " L'Art Japonais au XVIIIᵉ Siècle," which came out between 1891 and 1896, other European artists began experimenting in the Japanese manner. Amongst these was Sydney Lee, who became one of Mr. Morley Fletcher's, the English pioneer of this method, first disciples. It is, however, not in his colour prints done in this manner that Sydney Lee stands out as a truly original artist. His black and white is, in this regard, much more significant. In particular, such prints of his which were done in an undisguised glyptic white line have, in my opinion, more claim to be regarded as important. " The Limestone Rock," produced, according to Mr. Salaman's list, between 1904 and 1905 and hailed by that authority as an " example of landscape interpretation in the language of wood engraving comparable with fine landscape painting in the modern conception with its search for structural

82

expression," is mainly interesting on account of the artist's ingenious manipulation of *textures*. So also his large print [59], measuring 30 in. by 22 in., of "The Ravine" is remarkable as a piece of soft wood (sycamore) cutting with the knife. But the real "Sydney Lee" is to be seen in such prints as "The Windmill," "The Gatehouse" and "The Cottage Doorway" [60]; it is in such examples of xylography that originality in execution, if not necessarily in design or conception, is demonstrated. Aesthetically, Sydney Lee's prints are not as attractive as Nieuwenkamp's, with whose work they nevertheless have a superficial affinity, owing to the even distribution of black and white or light and shade values, which are in both cases diffused and not massed. With these two names we may fairly bring the survey of the pioneer era, so far as black and white in the European manner is concerned, to a close. Before tracing the further development of "black and white" xylography it is necessary to find and assign a place to the much better known and much more popular woodcut in colours.

From a Cut used by Grocers. English, late
XVIII. Century. Slightly reduced. [32]

From a woodcut by Pierre Gusman: "A Tivoli." 4¾×11½ in.

THE FIFTH CHAPTER: IN WHICH A PLACE IS ASSIGNED TO THE WOODCUT PRINTED IN SEVERAL COLOURS

IN its earliest intention the "black and white" formed, as we had seen, only the basis or "key" of a design of which colour was intended to be an integral part. The woodcut began merely as a device for the speedy and economical production of pictures, or at least picture substitutes. That this should be so is rather disturbing to our present-day conception of aesthetics : it offends indeed against our sensibility. The colour, which was in the early cuts applied by hand, nearly always partly obliterated or otherwise marred the effect of the drawing, and in book illustration broke the homogeneity of the typographical text and the illustration.

Colour, nevertheless, rather than the linear design, was the thing that was mainly desired and prized ; nor is this preference really remarkable since colour is the emotional, design the intellectual, element. The attraction and appeal of colour is immediate and physiological, not only peculiar to " the purest and most thoughtful minds," as Ruskin thought, but common to bird, beast, as well as man. The appeal of design which has to grow, both individually and racially speaking, out of time into understanding is slower, less forcible, but more insistent and more lasting. Design or drawing is, therefore, the higher quality of

84

From Charles Shannon's Chiaroscuro print : "The Porch." 5¼ in. diam. of printed surface.

the pictorial arts. Thus from the very fact that even in the oldest known woodcuts, discovered by Sir Aurel Stein, in Turkestan, the colour is applied sparingly, we must conclude, even without other evidence, that these cuts no longer represent a primitive phase of civilization, which latter, as we begin to realize more and more, is not to be regarded as a steady progress in every direction and at every moment, but as a succession of tidal waves now bearing this, now another, argosy of culture on its crests.

Not so much Altdorffer's ambitiously five-coloured print of the " Beautiful Virgin of Ratisbon," but rather Cranach's and Burgkmair's more limited and restrained achievements in colour-printing were aesthetically a step forward, because the colours were intended to heighten, by the addition of gold, silver, bluish grey and neutral tints, the aesthetic qualities of the cut. But there was no attempt at realism in the colouring of the " Beautiful Virgin," prints of which occur in differing colour schemes. Jobst de Negker, Burgkmair's printer, was further on the right lines with his brick red-tone plate and gilded armour of the Emperor Maximilian's portrait, although the gilding is as a species of high-light " heightening " suspiciously realistic. In his print of " Death the Strangler " the key block is, apparently, broken up and only does part duty for the deepest darks, the *linear* design being continued in the half-tones by another lighter coloured block, with the result that the tonal values of these earlier " Chiaroscuro " print anticipations are inferior to Ugo da Carpi's results achieved by the same process and which da Carpi registered as his own with the Signoria of Venice four years later (1516). Had the Chiaroscuro dispensed with the line block it might have developed into the Chinese method of producing colour prints, which has no contour or key block; as it is, it may have inspired the Japanese, who may possibly have seen some of these Italian prints, in which moreover there was frequently a bold pen-line contour. The aim of these Chiaroscuro prints in Renaissance hands, however, denoted a desire for greater realistic and illusional rather than decorative values. They, therefore, often resemble monochrome paintings of bas-reliefs, a category of subject that Mantegna began and the French decorators of the eighteenth century made popular. The aim then was to create an illusion of plastic actuality. The term " heightened " with white, applied to drawings and denoting the touches of "high-lights," is applicable likewise to Chiaroscuro prints, in which the effect is produced by removal of the surface from the tone

From Edvard Munch's woodcut : " Self Portrait."   6¾ × 4¼ in.   [69]

86

From Edvard Munch's woodcut: " The Death Chamber." $4\frac{1}{2} \times 5\frac{3}{8}$ in.   [70]

block in the spaces where the light, *i.e.*, the paper itself, shows in the print. By " heightening " the design a corresponding illusion of " depth " is produced, and it is this illusion of the third dimension which the " West," in diametrical opposition to the " East," cherished. There is a Chiaroscuro print by Ugo da Carpi [23] of the " Descent from the Cross " after Raphael, which, for triangularity of composition and plasticity of modelling, would have, and perhaps has, delighted the eye of Cézanne. In most cases, however, " Chiaroscuro " has neither the force of black and white nor the attractiveness and decorative value of the full palette. It is, indeed, a bastard process begotten out of light and colour values that are there nearly always in conflict. In modern times, Charles Shannon, with his series of " Twelve Months " and seasons, has produced results of greater aesthetic value, by reason of their finer, less illusional and more decorative treatment— they were intended for the decoration of china plates [61]—and greater restraint in handling.

87

Much more complicated and exceedingly efficient, though somewhat uninspired work, has been done in recent years by Gusman and J. Beltrand, and others, in France, and in Italy, Gino Barbieri, one of Italy's foremost traditional xylographers, has published some work of this kind printed in the magazine *Eroica,* which shows in design affinities in style with Greiner and Klinger, and other German draughtsmen. The earlier efforts of producing woodcuts in full colour were in Europe less successful than the Chiaroscuro prints and need here no mention, with one or two exceptions, and only because they displayed experimentally a new quality which the Japanese developed independently and with far better results.

J. B. Jackson attempted, in what he described as a " novissime excogitatum opus," to reproduce some Italian architectural landscapes in colour (1742), and in order to give the architecture concretely tactile values he went to the length of carving its sculptural figures, and other parts of masonry, in such a manner on the block that the print yielded under pressure a bas relief-like impression, of such depth (or from the obverse : height), as to cast shadows and reflect lights. [29B] John Skippe, a little later, seems to have had similar ideals in view in his " Leda and the Swan." The logical evolution of print-making with such ideals leads to the " bas-relief" photographs which enjoyed, some twenty years ago, a spell of popularity.

It is the merit of Eastern art to have weaned the European mind from such ideals of material realism and from such a conception of aesthetics. To Eastern conceptions, therefore, we must turn, not only in order to appreciate the modern European colour print, but also much of modern " black and white."

Curiously enough the Japanese colour printing, which was invented in China, began simultaneously with the development of the European colour print in the eighteenth century. The difference in conception, however, was fundamental. To the Oriental the painted picture was a reality in itself. To the Occidental mind it is an illusion of actuality and to be judged—at least by the majority—only in accordance with its illusional power ; or, as Bracquemont frankly put it : *" Par sa conception élementaire l'art de l'Extrême Orient est inférieur parcequ'il est incomplet dans la représentation de la nature."* [1]

If even the old Chinese painters prided themselves on their *realism* and were worshipped for their power of evoking illusions, these were not illusions of actuality. The dragons which they painted so realistically

---

[1] See *L'Image*, 1897, in an article on " La Gravure sur bois."

that they dare not give them eyes lest the animal should fly from the wall, no one had seen in " nature," and the tortures of hell which they painted so convincingly that the very sight of the painting made the spectators " sweat with fear,"[1] appealed of necessity only through the imagination, which indeed is the channel through which the pictorial emotions are generally reached. But the Renaissance exchanged emotional for intellectual appeals, personal vision for optic truth, emotional beauty for an aesthetic philosophic substitute.

Imagination was reared laboriously in libraries — Cimabue's "Madonna" was still an appeal; Botticelli's "Venus" already an argument, Velasquez' a demonstration of pictorial technique.

The West strives for three dimensional values, and seems to rest content only when it has represented the objects of its emotions until they look as if they could be weighed at the King's weigh-house or in a butcher's balance.

All such qualities are absent from Oriental art—even from its sculpture. A Buddha, in stone or in bronze, is not a realistic representation —but a poem; the solid material rises and falls like a wave in the ocean of space, a thought in the sea of potentiality slowly taking shape and sinking softly into the silence of nirvana.

We have then to temper our mind to a different harmony if we would understand, however imperfectly, the significance of Eastern art generally and the Japanese woodcut in particular. The perspective, both the optical and the spiritual one, differs. Unlike the Western painter, the Eastern artist looks down upon his picture from above, and since to him the picture space is a reality, and not merely the *vertical* pretext for an illusion of " Nature," it is *alive* from top to bottom, from side to side, from corner to corner. The objects that he represents cast no shadows, have no light and shade, since they are representations of ideas and not imitations of nature : as ideas they are real enough, but only the paper, the colours, the lines and the surfaces are actual, and it is with these actualities that the Japanese artist deals. From the earliest (seventeenth century) illustrated books, in which it is as doubtful as it is in early European woodcuts whether they were actually printed from wood or not, perhaps rather from metal or even brick, down to Hokusai and Hiroshige, who lived as late as 1858, we see the Japanese designer conceiving his picture surface as a vital unit, in which spacing, lines, colours and masses have

[1] See numerous examples of such " realism " quoted by Herbert A. Giles in his " Introduction to the History of Chinese Pictorial Art."

an aesthetic life, not, to be sure, *apart* from the subject significance of the picture, but of a wider and more general nature. Were this not so we should hardly be able to derive as much pleasure as we do, even from the Japanese woodcut, although its subject matter is, as a rule, less difficult to understand than the paintings in which even apparently simple subjects such as landscapes, flowers and animals have symbolic significance and poetic allusions, that are hardly translatable into Western conceptions.

What appeals to our eyes is the *pattern* of the Japanese print, and it is probably no mere coincidence that the creator of the Japanese woodcut, Moronobu (1638-1714), was a designer of textile patterns, the son of a father who was an embroiderer and of a grandfather who was a dyer. Moreover, Moronobu ended a gay life as a monk. This would seem to be a symbolic epitome of the forces that go to make the beauty of the Japanese print; at its best it is the expression of a mind sensitive above all, to rhythmic lines and the harmonic colours of the universe, and creating a " symphony " that includes for all its gaiety a note of renunciation.

Classic art in Europe despised all patterned drapery and saw the highest beauty only in naked human forms. The Japanese represent the nude seldom, and when they do so it is hardly ever its dignity that furnishes the theme of the representation. On the other hand, most of their figures are so enveloped in patterned draperies as to leave only the head exposed; even hands and feet are often concealed. As a consequence many prints that have for their subject only a single object—a wave, a mountain top, a figure, present a serene or sombre pattern to the eye, a picture moreover in which the lines of the drawing seem continuations of the calligraphic inscriptions without which no Japanese picture is really complete. These contour lines alone are, by reason of their stylistic rather than naturalistic significance, capable of making the most exquisite designs, in a manner still possible in the early European design, but which there the growing naturalism of the Renaissance gradually and completely destroyed. One need only compare the treatment of clouds and water in the Japanese and early German woodcuts to see how nearly the Eastern symbolic conception once agreed with that of the West. As regards the technical quality of the line, we find that it is both in the East as it was in Europe, a facsimile cut and, therefore, essentially reproductive: only the Japanese use a brush in lieu of a pen. Moreover, they employed, since Tanaka Masunobu in the middle of the eighteenth century, the *white* line

90

From a woodcut, "Le Ruisseau," by Gabriel Belot. 11 ×8 in.

cut, to be distinguished from the much older "negative" rubbings taken from engraved stones and of Chinese invention. As the Japanese derived their culture and with it their manner of writing, and so also of drawing, from China, so they also learnt the art of printing in several colours from their greater neighbours. There are beautiful Chinese colour prints of the seventeenth century, printed in many colours and without any black or outline drawing, but they are, we learn, reproductions of pictures rather than original inventions. In the forties of the eighteenth century Okumura Masanobu is said to have invented the art of printing in more than one colour and beni (saffron pink) and soruko (grass green) were added to the black; until then the colours had been applied by hand. Printing with an unlimited number of different colours dates from the year 1765, and of this full-blown colour print Harunobu is the leading master. He it was who introduced the beautiful harmonies of secondary and tertiary colours (for instance, olive, pink, grey, salmon pink, dark green, orange and yellow); he, too, invented the black background, the pictorial lusciousness of which some of our younger academicians have only recently discovered; and he finally added "blind" printing (i.e., a pattern impressed on the paper in inverted relief, but without colour) as a further aesthetic allurement to his representations of beautiful women.

This Harunobu School of the woodcut, with its exuberant chromatic scale, was followed by the School of Shun-sho, which, though more reticent in colour, first introduced gold leaf and mica powder as new means of physical attraction to the prints. Popular and fashionable actors and half-actresses, as well as beautiful women of the Yoshiwara, formed the subject matter of these woodcuts.

The head and culmination of this XVIII. Century School was the pupil of Kyonaga, Utamaro, whose prints did more than any other's to make the Japanese woodcut known and prized in Europe. By a curious coincidence, Utamaro flourished at about the same period as Bewick, his "Ehon momochidori's," or Book of Birds, being published in 1789, Bewick's "British Birds" coming out eight years later. But if Bewick was mainly an engraver, with a mind dominated by the associative values of a subject, Utamaro was entirely an artist to whom sea shells, insects and landscapes were as aesthetically interesting as the doings of the Yoshiwara.

Since it is not our purpose to give an historic account of the Japanese woodcut, we will only mention Toyokunis' name, as that of the

92

From a woodcut by Emile Pissarro. $3\frac{7}{8} \times 6\frac{1}{4}$ in.

founder of a great eclectic school of woodcut artists, who adopted
Kyonaga's and Shun-sho's and Utamaro's styles, and thus became
one of the most celebrated masters of the Ukiyo-e School, which
corresponds in matter, though not in manner, to our realistic and
impressionistic schools of painting.
But the greatest of all Shun-sho's pupils is that wonderful eccentric old
man Hokusai, who was born in 1760 and died in 1849, the last of the
great Japanese woodcutters, regarded as a plebeian and vulgar realist
in the eyes of his compatriots, a calumny which his "Great Wave"
alone, if nothing else, would contradict. "So universal indeed is the
achievement of Hokusai," said Sir Charles Holmes nearly twenty-five
years ago now, "that the painter who can learn nothing from a careful
study of his prints must either be unfit for his trade or a greater genius
than any the world has hitherto known." But what was his particular
significance? There is only one word to express it, and that is:
vision. It was not what he saw, not beautiful women, not popular
actors, not indeed any associative matter that made his pictures of
every-day life, of wind and water, snow and rain, gods or ghosts,
beautiful or interesting; it was his way of seeing, his way of arranging

93

what he saw on his wood block [62], and his way of selecting the lines and the colours of his vision so that you should see what he meant you to see.

It is because his subjects are, for the most part, so near to our own experience, depend so little on acquaintance with their associative matter, that his work and that of his follower, Hiroshige, demonstrates to European eyes more clearly than that of other Orientals the lesson implied in all Oriental art and once also in that of the West, namely, that the foundation of the visual arts is VISION, not optics, spirit, not matter. I have dealt with the history of the Japanese colour print rather more fully than I intended because it is based on this important difference in vision.

The enthusiasm raised by the appearance of the Hokusais and Utamaros and Oriental art generally in Europe, and fanned by European aesthetics, such as the Goncourts, into the sacrificial flame of a veritable cult, has had important and unforeseen consequences for Western art in general, and for the woodcut in particular. The Japanese manner of designing in map-like spaces and printing from the plank by rubbing with the " baren " or a substitute for this " pad," by means of which flat tones of one or—by superimposition of several blocks— of many colours are obtained, became general. Coming as it did, when advanced and experimentally inclined artists were filled with impressionist light theories, we find the Japanese manner running in harness with impressionism. The Western school of colour-xylography, in so far as it is founded on the practices of the *fin de siècle*, presents therefore, a mixture of Eastern and Western elements. Emil Orlik went to Japan in the early nineties in order to learn the " tricks of the trade " ; but so far as I know the most important trick is not practised or recommended by the European professors of the craft : *viz.*, a strict division of labour between designer, cutter and printer. On the other hand, the Japanese method has been carefully studied with a view to exploitation in conjunction with Western scientific processes, and in order to perfect what Mr. Morley Fletcher calls "the wonderful and excellent work that is produced to-day by machinery." Mr. Morley Fletcher, in conjunction with Mr. J. D. Batten, is the pioneer of the Japonesque colour print in England. Mr. Allen E. Seaby [63A] is their colleague and coadjutor. The British, as well as the Continental artists, have all produced admirable prints without, with partial, or, as Mr. William Giles, with exclusive employment of metal plates. Other artists of the multiple colour print are, in

94

From Hokusai's woodcut in colour : "Kirifuri Fall." (B.146). $14\frac{1}{2} \times 10\frac{7}{8}$ in. [62]

The Duke of Marlborough

I farm 5000 to 6000 acres myself without a manager since he has gone to the war.

I have ploughed up hundreds of acres of land I have already planted over 1000 acres of winter crops. I think I shall plant 1000 acres of barley & 1000 acres of oats before we hear the cuckoo

This is not a bad effort for one citizen

From a woodcut by Ludovic Rodo: A satire on words reported to have been spoken by the present Duke, during the war. $7\frac{3}{4} \times 5\frac{1}{2}$ in.

[74]

England, Mrs. Austen Brown, Miss Ethel Kirkpatrick, Miss Edith Richards and Miss Mabel Royds, whose work [63c] deserves special mention because it combines with the Oriental technique a very European, original and personal sense of colour and composition. Further, there are to be named, J. E. Platt, Hall Thorpe, E. A. Verpilleux and the late Charles Mackie [63]: the latter pursuing aims which are imitative of other media, with quite singular success, the former using the press, instead of the hand, for the production of his prints.

It is not, however, my purpose here to discuss the technical merit of laborious processes, more particularly as I disagree fundamentally with such a statement as this made by Mr. Fletcher[1] :

" The best of all the wonderful and excellent work that is produced to-day by machinery is that which bears evidence in itself of its derivation from arts under the pure conditions of classic craftsmanship, and shows the influence of their study."

Our machine-made work is so *bad* fundamentally and radically *because* it bears this very evidence. The aesthetic value in machine-made work is in the exact proportion of its *dissimilarity* to hand-wrought work ; the machine-made thing should not look as if it were made by hand, nor the hand-made thing as if it had been made by machinery. The popular standards of to-day imply the very reverse ; the hand is praised for mechanical virtues and the machine for the " artistic " qualities of its productions.

For such reasons I am as greatly impressed with the ingenuity and assiduity displayed in many modern colour " processes," including wood and metal cuts, as I am unconvinced of their aesthetic importance. The more ingenious, exact and complicated the " process " the greater the curb it puts on the force and spontaneity of creative expression— so long as the aim is imitative of hand-made qualities. The creative artist who will use the machine *in lieu* of his hand for the purpose of *creative* design has not yet arrived.

The great activity which commenced at the turn of this century in colour woodcut has borne no fruit of any *considerable* aesthetic value : most of these things are no more then superficially pleasing and decorative from the aesthetic, though often highly ingenious from the technical point of view.

This also holds good not only of Baxter's, but other coloured hard wood engraving methods. Some of the best work of this kind are the

[1]" Wood Block Printing," by F. Morley Fletcher, London, 1916.

96

From the woodcut in colour by Charles H. Mackie : " The Doge's Palace, Venice." $17\frac{1}{4} \times 21\frac{1}{2}$ in.

[63]

From the woodcut in colour by Mabel Royds : " The Housetop."

From a woodcut, "Five o'clock," by Ludovic Rodo.   5¾ × 7 in.   [75]

engravings by Albert Kruger, after old masters such as Holbein and Signorelli; but they are purely reproductive and, therefore, only of technical interest. Excellent reproductive work on soft wood in the Japanese manner is being done by a native of that country, Urushibara, in London. His reproductions of Brangwyn's water-colours [64] and of his own designs, necessitating numberless printings, are admirable, but for Europeans constitutionally " inimitable "—that is to say: not to be imitated.

Although the Japanese manner in conjunction with impressionistic design has been practised throughout Europe, its xylographic results have been less significant than their influence upon the artist's conception of design. Amongst the best Continental work as interesting in design and cutting as they are in printing are the landscapes and interiors [65] produced by Fräulein Margarethe Geibel, of Weimar. Her interiors of the Goethe Haus and the Grandducal Palace are quite remarkable. They seem to be done with a minimum of effort and a maximum of effect which yet is neither reproductive nor Japonesque. On the other hand, such colour prints as the " Vues de Paris," by Léon Bonfils, hover between European and Eastern conceptions. They are designed in line on hard wood, like his black-and-white cuts, but with the addition of flat Japanese colour planes. In the example here illustrated [65B] one can trace the linear convention of contours of Western tradition, and the pictorial draughtsmanship of the Impressionists, the former in the treatment of the architecture generally, the latter in the tonal treatment of the quays and their reflections. Side by side with these European methods we find a superficially Japonesque composition and the flat decorative colour in sky and water and in the green of the trees: but here certain flicks of high light betray the European mind which aims at plastic relief.

All this is the effect of the new freedom which the modern artists have gained, compared with their tradition-bound forbears, but which carries with it obligations that are not yet clearly recognized and admitted.

It is to an analysis of "this new freedom" which we must therefore now turn.

98

From J. B. Jackson's woodcut in colour: "View of Roman Ruins after Marco Ricci." 16½ × 23 in.

From Léon Bonfils' woodcut in colour : "Le Pont Neuf." $7\frac{5}{8} \times 9\frac{3}{8}$ in.

[65B]

From the woodcut in colour by M. Geibli : " Mansard Room, Gœthe Haus, Weimar."

[65]

From Urushibara's woodcut in colour, after Brangwyn's water-colour : "The Devil's Bridge." 14¼ × 20 in.

From a woodcut by Galanis. 2 ×7½ in.

THE SIXTH CHAPTER: INTRODUCING THE PATHFINDERS OF THE NEW FREEDOM FROM THE FETTERS OF EXHAUSTED TRADITIONS

SO far-reaching, so radical indeed is the change in outlook that has gradually come over art since the last hundred years that there are many, not only among the public, but among the artists themselves, who are still unable to see its justification, still less its drift. The change, however, has nevertheless been gradual, and artists who have themselves contributed their share to bringing it about may be found on the side of the scoffers even to-day. In the circumstances, it seems to me advisable to illustrate the nature of the change with one of its earliest, undoubted, and yet little recognized phenomena, even though I would appear to be digressing and have to make an excursion into another medium.

Ever since the early Renaissance the artist's aim had been to create an illusion of nature, or in other words, to make his natural objects —animal, vegetable and mineral—as imitative and convincing as possible, even when this involved the transformation of a Madonna into a Venus, or the degradation of a Christ into an Adonis. The method by which such metamorphoses were effected was based on " nature study " modified by classical formulæ. That the artist's composition was regulated by considerations which had no reference to the subject matter of his " illusional representation " was only recognized by the great masters themselves whom the followers copied. The public knew nothing of this and continued to judge a work of art firstly by the subject in general, and secondly by its conception of " beauty " in details. The more scientifically accurate representation became, that

99

is to say the more illusional accuracy was desired, the less attention was given to the fact that pictorial *composition* is in itself a contradiction of illusion. Nature cannot be *composed* because it is not *static*; a work of art must be composed because it must be static—*i.e.*, self-contained.[1]

Composition in art means a re-ordering of objects as they are found in nature—it involves a disturbance of their natural order. Representations of natural facts which appear in a work of art are, therefore, always subject to conditions which are not those of *nature*. A work of art is then quite definitely not an accurate representation, copy or imitation of nature.

An illustration will make this more clear. When Whistler affixed his " Butterfly " signature to his canvases, he was doing a very remarkable thing, a thing that not only conflicted with the conscious or subconscious art theories of that time, but strangely enough with the artist's own.

In Whistler's theory, as indeed in that of the majority, the picture-frame is a " window " or a doorway, opening on to an illusion of a space *behind* it. The spectator, according to this theory, shared by Ruskin, looks into the depths of the illusionary scene before his eyes, as it were *through* the canvas. In other words, the picture surface is regarded as invisible. In spite of his metaphorical use of language by which he poetically termed his pictures " symphonies " and " arrangements," Whistler became so logical and uncompromising a materialist and realist that he ceased to paint anything from imagination except —his " butterfly " signature, and it is this which indicates that his aesthetic instinct was superior to his logic. Whistler's butterfly signature has nothing to do with his " subjects," nor is it in any way connected with illusional requirements, but it is a very essential part of his composition. It is clear, therefore, that the artist never actually looked *through* the surface of the canvas, but on the contrary very carefully *at* it, because he put his signature where there was nothing amiss with the *illusion*, but something missing on the actuality of space, *i.e.*, the canvas. Whistler's butterfly was, on his canvases (not so truly on the margin of his etchings), an intruder from Japan. His pictorial monogram, affixed as it was to the picture plane, has more kinship with the " vase " sign of a Shun-sho, than with the " cartellino " one

[1]Even the Time Arts—Music and Poetry—are " static " in the sense that a " piece " of music or of poetry is a condition of sounds that cannot be disturbed without destroying the work of art, which is perceived by us as such because of the *condition* it puts our mind in, making it *static* in relation to the time of the outside world.

100

From a woodcut by Emile Bernard for " Chansons de France."   Original size.   [76]

encounters on Venetian paintings or the " trade mark " tablet with Dürer's monogram seen on his prints. Whistler's enthusiasm for Japanese composition led him more and more away from European composition into a contradictory Japonesque decorativeness, exemplified by raised or double horizons, or all but blank spaces and quite un-European marginal interests. Nevertheless, Whistler's " conceits " serve as an early and significant milestone on the road which art was to take. So long as we continue to look in the Western manner at pictures as substitutes of nature, art is at best like a vegetarian banquet with its " mock-turkey " and nut meat " sausages " and ginger-wine, a feast—*faute de mieux*.

To judge a picture, not as a substitute for, or as an illusion of, something else, but as an actuality and a reality, this conception of the function of art would probably never have arisen in the West but for the arrival of the Japanese colour prints. In these prints the subject or meaning was, to us, obscured, nature strangely " distorted," but the aesthetic qualities for these very reasons all the more obvious.

The arrival of the Japanese colour print marks the introduction of the thin end of the ever-widening wedge that is being driven between the representational and the aesthetic significance of art.

The breach opened the more readily as Impressionism, that is to say, the arrest of the fleeting moment, was an aim that held both linear contour and subject significance in slight esteem.

It will be noticed that extremes began to meet: the flat all over vertical composition and the recessional horizontal perspective found their amalgamation in Whistler, their culmination in Cézanne, who endeavoured to give Impressionism a firm structure and organization in the composition of vertical aspect and horizontal perspective.

However the honours be divided between such things as decorativeness, solidity, representational and abstract truth, the greatest and most important gain to art is the knowledge that a work of art is a reality and not a substitute for, or an imitation of, Nature. One can legitimately dispute about the value of the many new " isms " that have, with mushroom energy, sprung from this knowledge, so long as one realizes that a work of art can be judged, if at all, only by the relation of its parts to *its own* whole, and of the whole to one's own feelings, intelligence and experience, but not by any external and objective facts. Neither Whistler nor Cézanne made use of the wood block as a means of putting their views of art to the test of black and white. The wood engravings of Whistler's drawings have little xylographic

From a woodcut by Carlègle for " L'Anthologie Grecque." 4 × 3 in. [78]

value; much less in fact than Rossetti's, Millais', Leighton's and Sandys' designs. That is only natural, since Whistler was too feminine a draughtsman; but one wonders that Cézanne was not tempted to try his virile and all too heavy hand at a craft which lends itself to bold adventures in form and the quintessence of colours : black and white. The new path was, however, opened by a finder now closely associated with this " primitive."

At about the time when the English Ricketts and Shannon were seeking an escape from academic dullness, impressionistic instability and the commercial sordidness of life in general by a flight into fifteenth century Italy : and when the Czech, Emil Orlik, from similar motives sought to wrest the secret of the Japanese colour print from its makers by a visit to Japan, a strange half-European, prompted by similar discontent, fled to the South seas, hoping there to heal the fissures of his soul amongst gentle savages. This paradoxical quest led, as it was bound to do, to personal failure, but it helped to give to Western art a fresh outlook and a new direction.

Gauguin deliberately set himself against tradition. " In art," he said, " there are only revolutionists or plagiarists," a profoundly mistaken notion, since revolutions in art are always gradual, the origins obscure and not to be traced to individuals. Raphael, Dürer and Rembrandt are each a culmination—an end as well as a beginning, and neither the one nor the other in an absolute sense.

103

The spirit which drove Gauguin to the South seas, Orlik to Japan and Ricketts to the Quattrocento, was one and the same seeking its liberation by different means. Exotic and " revolutionary " as Gauguin's work looks, it implies by its very form and nature that against which it protests. Gauguin possessed, as he well knew himself, a rare instinct for beauty, and it is this instinct which makes his work acceptable and partly comprehensible to us. But the fundamental *failure*, the incurable fissure where there should be wholeness, passion where there should be love, tempest where there should be calm, will keep his work in the category of significant attempt rather than perfect achievement. He will be regarded by future *historians* with Cézanne and others, as one of the primitives of the new vision in art. A curious light is thrown on his immediate failure to make his supposedly " primitive " art consonant with the really primitive mind, by the manner in which a number of his wood blocks were found years after his death in Tahiti. It appears that the Czecho-Slovak Minister of War, Stefanik,[1] made the acquaintance of Gauguin's native wife in Tahiti, whither Stefanik had gone in his capacity of astronomer in order to watch an eclipse of the sun. This acquaintance led to the discovery of Gauguin blocks which the woman and her family had preserved out of a regard for the useful rather than the beautiful : the wood was in fact used to repair a pig-trough and a garden fence. These blocks were no doubt cut in his house, which contained this motto : *Te Faruru*, in polite French : " *Ici on fait l'amour.*" *Sic vos non vobis meltificates apes!* How much indeed depends on the material supplied by the artist's exotic environment itself, rather than on his " revolutionary " spirit, is realizable if we compare his Breton with his Tahiti subjects. Possibly the artist may have developed, and his instinct for beauty may have received the stimulus it required, but there is no doubt that these Tahitian cuts are aesthetically more satisfying. Gauguin's use of a colour block,[2] *e.g.*, orange in " Te Faruru " and " Te Maruru," a fiery red in " Te Alua," is sensuously exciting, but even the severe black and white becomes a thing of sensuous beauty, which the spectator realizes in a superficial manner : really to understand Gauguin one must read his story " Noa Noa," shortly to be issued by his friend, Daniel de Monfreid, in its entirety. It contains in its manuscript, besides drawings, water-colours; also a number of woodcuts.

[1] See Zpravy Volnych Smeru, 1919. Published in Prague.
[2] It appears that there are woodcuts in colour in existence which were not signed by Gauguin, and which his son expressly declines to recognize as authentic.

104

From a woodcut by Paul Gauguin: "Mahna no varua ino," one of a series of ten woodcuts entitled "Noa-Noa." 8 × 14 in. [67]

From a woodcut by Paul Gauguin: "L'Univers est crée," one of a series of ten woodcuts entitled "Noa-Noa." 8×14 in.

[68]

Most people will see in his cuts only grotesque designs and savage idiosyncrasies. Nevertheless, it is the freedom and mastery with which the artist uses both tool and material [67, 68][1] that makes them truly remarkable. By mastery is here not implied a skill acquired by apprenticeship and long practice, but rather a natural gift of instinctive knowledge, a sheer will to make tool and material yield him what *he* wanted, irrespective of conventions. With Gauguin it is never a case of incapacity in execution. His cuts, therefore, are of intense interest technically: he uses white line on the "plank"; he scrapes; he makes play with the natural grain of the wood, but without borrowing methods or effects from Japan. In Gauguin's method of cutting there is infinitely more "art" or inventive craftsmanship, though not as much "genius" as there is in Blake's; but in both cases it means that craftsmanship is the obedient servant of expression.

Whether Edvard Munch [69], some three or four years later, was directly influenced by Gauguin, I cannot say, but his work startled at least the Continental world as much as the Frenchman's. Munch's, at the time incomprehensible, pictorial utterance caused a sensation on the Continent, where it was repudiated violently even by the *advanced* painters who had become impressionists, and it ultimately caused in Germany the "Secession," a society of the more revolutionary artists, out of which eventually a great part of expressionistic art was to develop. Like Gauguin, Munch was an individualist. The things he represents in his paintings, his lithographs and his woodcuts are his personal reactions against life. Whereas impressionism taught the artist to efface himself, to react as it were purely mechanically and objectively against the manifestations of light and the modifications of colour, Munch, like Gauguin, on the contrary, subjected the visual forms of the world entirely to his emotional reactions. So far the parallel with Gauguin is complete. But whereas the Frenchman's message was a Rousseau-like protest against civilization, Munch's was an Ibsenesque evaluation; he, like Ibsen, remains throughout a modern European, an analyst of the European's "psyche." As a consequence Munch's art is not decorative, which Gauguin—in spite of his attempted exploration of the native's soul—is above all. With the Norwegian, implied, associative values count more than aesthetic values. So, for example, an apparently simple representation of a bedroom turns out to be a scene in a *death chamber* [70]; the likeness of a woman seated on

[1]Exact information as to the artist's woodcuts has proved difficult to obtain, and though it is now on the way it will be too late for inclusion in these pages.

her bed is called "*Night*," but the picture no less than the title implies the tragedy that is visible only through the inner eye.

In his woodcuts we find Norwegian equivalents to Gauguin's " Te Faruru " such as "The Kiss," a subject that "intrigued" him with several versions in etching and painting : " Man and Woman," "Jealousy," " Melancolia." Often he repeats in woodcut what he has expressed in another medium, but always modified in composition and design to meet the altered conditions. He uses two methods. In one he allows the wood as such to " speak " in the flat Japanese manner, so that the grain of the wood forms an intentional part in the design, whilst the figures are simplified to almost symbolic simplicity. These cuts he also prints in several simple colours. In his black and white woodcuts, however, the gouge chips away the wood after the manner of the primitives, with this difference, that impressionism and emphasis on light values has taught him to design white on black ; like Gauguin's, Munch's approach to the woodcut is no longer " calligraphic " or translative as with most of the work we have hitherto considered, but entirely direct, the tool itself fashioning like Gauguin's the design in the cutting ; like Gauguin's, too, it subordinates representational values entirely to the artist's requirements. The hand that executes is controlled consciously by the inner eye ; I say consciously, because unconsciously it is always the inner eye that is in control, though it has taken man untold centuries to become conscious of this truth.

It was Blake who established this duality of vision and Gauguin and Munch who first confirmed it ; therein lies their importance, for in the truly modern woodcut it is tool and material which together pronounce the message the artist has to convey, but which they neither " interpret," " translate," nor even primarily multiply.

We arrive thus at the craft of woodcutting as an autonomous art.

From Vivien Gribble's woodcut illustration for "Sixe Idillia."
5 × 5¼ in.   [77]

THE SEVENTH CHAPTER: DEALING WITH THE PRESENT CONSERVATIVE LINEAR TREATMENT OF THE DESIGN

GAUGUIN and Munch established the artist's right to make use of the wood block for the purpose of aesthetic expression in *any* manner he might think conducive to his ends. Xylography thus quite definitely ceased to be merely a means for the reproduction or interpretation of *other* methods of design.

This right, I repeat, is not, as yet, generally recognized. The majority of the public have no interest in xylography or, for that matter, in any other form of aesthetic expression as such; they still look above all for an imitation of " nature." Even amongst the artists there are still a great number who consciously or unconsciously demand of xylography graphic and chalcographic rather than xylographic qualities. They think in *lines* and in terms of imitation, *i.e.*, of a design originated by pen or pencil, or even by brush, rather than by the material and the cutting tool. " Modern " aesthetic ideas and theories have,

107

From a woodcut by Carlègle for " Daphnis et Chloe." $4\frac{1}{4} \times 3\frac{1}{2}$ in.
[79]

nevertheless, influenced some of these " traditionalists," so that the line of demarcation is not always clearly definable, and one cannot speak in absolute terms of *creative* and *reproductive* craftsmen. The case of Auguste Lepère is an interesting one in point. This craftsman's earlier tone engravings, though they suggested reproductions of water-colour and oil paintings, were, in fact, *technically* more original than his later cuts, which are really more or less complicated facsimiles of drawings. So also his compatriots and part contemporaries, such as P. E. Colin, Pierre Gusman [71], Vibert, Perrichon, and several more of the professional and highly skilled craftsmen can hardly be said to be creative xylographers, even when they essay independent expression. Both Gusman and Colin resort to a method of striation which is a survival of the metal engraver's technique. The basis of Vibert's work is the pen and ink drawing, whilst there are instructive studies of trees [72] by Gabriel Belot which are, in essentials, not different from the old woodcutter's "G.G.N." facsimile pen drawing.

108

From the woodcut in colour by Allen E. Seaby: "The Halcyon."

[63ᴀ]

From a design by " Vox," engraved by Marie Ariel for " Les Marguérites
sont effuillées." 4 × 4 in. [80]

One of Lucien Pissarro's brothers, Paul Emile, practises various
manners, most of them, like the one here illustrated [73], likewise
based on the pen line, but of late he is attempting to give his cuts a
more properly xylographic aspect. Another brother of Lucien's, and
Paul Emile's senior, Ludovic Rodo, is distinguished by his keen
sense of humour which causes his clever and facile work, " woodier "
in execution than in design, to display a strongly associative interest.
The " Duke of Marlborough " [74] is a satirical comment on a speech
made by the present Duke as reported, so the artist tells me, in one of
the daily papers during the " Great War." The other cut is a French
rendering of that typically English institution " le fiffoclock " [75].
In same cases the pen line basis of the woodcut is obvious ; in others
there seems often plain evidence of the *directly* cut design.
Appearances in this respect are often deceptive. Emile Bernard, for
instance, has a number of excellent illustrative cuts to his credit, but
their xylographic *bona fides* is not clear. His illustrations to

" Chansons de France " [76] and Villon's Ballads are endowed, by a system of short hatchings, with a quality which looks like the natural method of the old cutter, but is, nevertheless, here not a technical characteristic, but an artificial and *aesthetic* conceit. The evolution of this technique into one of thoroughly glyptic appearance is displayed in his three illustrations for a sonnet—" Le Départ," by Jean Dorsal.[1] In these cuts one can see the reed-pen design progressively disappearing in each successive subject under the attack of the graver, the third cut being strongly suggestive of the wooden material and the cutting tool —which latter appears in the first illustration as a self-effacing slave of the reed-pen line. If I am correctly informed, the technique, however, is due entirely to the cutter who, despite appearances, is not Monsieur Bernard.

The fact that this separation of designing and cutting is possible, much more than the difference of identity between cutter and designer, marks cuts and engravings of this kind off from the truly *creative* modern work. Into this category of uncreative design we must place the able cuts of the Rouquet family, Auguste, Achille and Jeanne, which appear to be founded on ordinary pen drawings, just as Gabriel Belot's tree study and Bernard's illustration were founded on reed or broad-nibbed pen drawings.

In England, Miss Vivien Gribble has made an attempt in the page decorations [77] for the "Sixe Idillia" edition, published by Duckworths, to conventionalize the black line so that it assumes an almost inflexible character presumed to be in keeping with the hard-wood block. Apart from the typographical problem upon which I will touch presently, Miss Gribble's formula seems to me too rigid; in her "Rabbits in the Corn,"[2] the formula is combined with the "white" line and with a much better aesthetic sense. But the black line, which stands for colour, and the white line, which stands for light, are seen to be at variance in her cut "Milking."[2]

In this contradiction of means, however, the English artist is in good company. Carlègle, the Swiss xylographer, though a much more experienced draughtsman, employs like her a technique the foundation of which is the draughtsman's black line, and like her he uses it for " classic " compositions. But to his black line figures he adds white line " staffage." Carlègle is so accomplished an artist, so inventive and delightful in his compositions, that only the sensitive eye discovers in

[1] In No. 3—*Le Nouvel Imagier*.
[2] Reproduced in " Contemporary English Woodcuts," Duckworth, 1922.

110

ARCHITECTURES

TOME PREMIER

From a Frontispiece designed and cut in wood by Paul Vera. 16 × 11 in.   [81]

his illustrations an occasional clash between the white and the black line forces. Amongst the books illustrated by him I mention the following : " La fille d'Auberge Copa " after Vergil, " Les plus jolies roses de l'Anthologie Grecque," [78] " Les amours pastorales de Daphnis et Chloe " [79]. This latter title recalls the earlier " Daphnis et Chloe " illustrations by Shannon and Ricketts, and offers interesting points for comparison. The earlier work is much more literal, literary and calligraphic and forms much more successfully an *integral* part of the printed page, whereas Carlègle's designs, with their greater plastic and pictorial qualities, must be regarded as decorative adjuncts to the text.

Artists who use a great deal of black line in conjunction with white line and additional colour are two very able collaborators, Maximilian Vox and his wife " Marie Ariel," who sometimes cuts her husband's designs. Their illustrations in a serial publication : " Le Jardin de Candide," embracing amongst others, the " Fragments d'une traduction nouvel d'Hérodote," Montesquieu's " Dialogue de Sylla et Eucarte," " Le Comte Pacha de Berneval " and in " Les Marguérites sont effeuillées " [80] show, in spite of the somewhat hard and unglyptic quality of the black line in skilful combination with colours, much originality of design.

Another Parisian artist who makes extensive use of the black line, but whose designs are by reason of their cubistic or rather geometric formula [81, 82] both more " modern " and more organically part of the printed page, is Paul Vera. Vera's typographical decorations have just the *open* quality, the right weight and linear character which makes them properly the calligraphic counterpart of the letter type.

We touch here upon a very important question which deserves ventilation at this point, *viz.*: the function and suitability of the woodcut for the illustration of modern books.

The particular mechanical advantage of the " cut " is, of course, the possibility of printing it together with the text ; whereas the copper and steel engravings and lithographs have to be printed separately. This homogeneity does not, however, in itself produce a unity. One may see this if one studies such an excellent wood engraving as that of Menzel's illustrations for the " History of Frederick the Great " [37]. Here the connection between text and illustration is purely associative, or literary, but not aesthetic.

The modern " book beautiful " is a distinctly English creation. Before, in the early " Nineties," the " Kelmscott," the " Vale," the

" Essex House " and the (Anglo-French) " Eragny " presses were established, the illustrations were habitually inserted, or introduced, into the text with which they had no formal connection at all. They were generally " vignetted," an absurd misnomer, since the original "vignettes" were of course very firmly designed ornamental borders of vine—symbolical of " Faith "—which framed the pages of illuminated manuscripts. The very nature of these misnamed vignettes, a cloudy dissolution of the design into the white of the page, militated against any firm structural connection with the printed text. This nearly always ugly manner of inserting illustrations had become increasingly popular from the seventeenth century onwards.

William Morris and Charles Ricketts, though prompted by a sentimental, Victorian "Oh for the touch of a vanished hand" feeling, gave the printed page a unity and architectural compactness which, as a conscious aesthetic effort, was unprecedented.

These reformers found it necessary to re-introduce or redesign special old forms of type, some of it, however, like Ricketts' Kings' type, not specially attractive, legible or homogeneous in form. Pissarro added the further device of printing his illustrations in a colour-scale that would *tone* with the colour weight of the page. The " Beaumont Press " has recently followed these ideas up by a delightful edition of Goldoni's " The Goodhumoured Ladies " illustrated by Ethelbert White, whose, in themselves excellent, woodcuts however only preserve the unity of the page because they are not printed in black. Craig and Nicholson, who were not afraid of heavy blacks in the cut, counter weighted these by a very black letter.

All these English efforts are thoroughly consistent. That in the " building " of a book page, in so far as it is meant to be an aesthetic and not a merely technical enterprise, illustration and text should be considered as part of a single unit, is a fact by no means generally appreciated. When one for example glances through " L'Image," of the nineties, and through " Le Nouvel Imagier," of 1914 to 1920, one is struck with the inferiority of conception, even in the case of the best French woodcutters in this particular respect. The very title page of " Le Nouvel Imagier," by Lepère, is a purely literal illustration with no decorative qualities ; the lettering, both in design and spacing is—*sans phrase*—bad. As regards the specimens of book " making," only very few of the examples given can be said to have succeeded. Amongst these exceptions are Laboureur's " Deux Dialogues des Dieux de Lucien," [83] in the first number ; F. Siméon's " Le Vin,"

T

From Adolfo de Karolis' woodcut decorations for D'Annunzio's "Figlio di Jorio." Original size. [85, 86]

by Vion d'Alibrey, in the second, and the already mentioned Emile Bernard in the third number.

The failure is, however, not surprising considering the special problem "Le Nouvel Imagier" set out to solve. "*Chaque artiste chargé d'orner un texte*" it explained, "*a donc decidé du choix des caractères selon le style de ses bois.*" This is modern individualism defeating itself. Under the conditions here given the type existed already before the illustrations were made, consequently, the only rational thing would have been to choose the character of the illustration in accordance with an already existing font, and not *vice versa*.

Since, however, other than purely aesthetic considerations govern the design of fonts, and since in any case the fonts are cut in metal, there seems to be no valid reason why the woodcut should, in our days, be used in conjunction with the type. A page on which the illustration is a calligraphic continuation of the calligraphic, though metal-cut, character is the only one aesthetically justifiable, and such illustrations can, as a rule, be produced by the pen and reproduced by the camera more faithfully and more economically.

The woodcut as a modern form of book-illustration is—one reluctantly concludes—a mere sentimentality, unless the artist finds in the technique itself a more aesthetic—compare Vera [81, 82]—or a more potent—compare Masereel [179] of whom more later—means of expression.

This brings us to another point one has to consider in this connection: the associative relation of the style of design with the text.

Intellectual artists such as, for example, Ricketts, tend to substitute associative emotions for aesthetic emotions: it is because they regard the Renaissance (or any other period or place) as a "charmed time in the development of man" that they attempt "to evolve what one might imagine as possible in

114

From Francesco Nonni's woodcut : " Il Pino."   8¼ × 5 in.   [87]

one charmed moment or place." If one examines such specimens of typographical design and decoration as Gray's "Spiritual Poems" [46] or "The World at Auction," or even the very first book, "Hero and Leander" [45] with an unbiassed mind one becomes aware that one's pleasure springs almost entirely from associative thoughts. As designs they do not "hang" together in linear or in mass rhythms. However excellent in details and in technical qualities, and in that respect the "Spiritual Poems" are quite remarkable, the *unit* is only realizable by an intellectual [1] but not by a direct aesthetic emotion.

In "Le Nouvel Imagier," Gusman ornaments "Textes Classiques Anciens" with a classic vase "motif," obviously because he regards the Greek vase as such as classic ; just as he regards his design of figures as classic because they are nude or half draped.

This too is a legacy of the Renaissance which confuses in an increasing degree accuracy and literal with aesthetic truth. It is not facts such as Greek vases or draped figures which ensure classicity, but the *spirit* in which such or other things are designed.

If Gusman's cuts fail from this point of view, there are other more able and original artists—I am not speaking here of craftsmanship, Gusman is the *doyen* of professional wood engravers in France—whose work can yet not be reckoned amongst the truly modern.

There is, for example, some Italian work printed in the "Eroica" which links up with the Vale press and the Kelmscott group in style. Adolfo de Karolis, an otherwise independent classicist, with a style of engraving in the technique of Scolari, has illustrated d'Annunzio's "Figlio di Jorio" with cuts that might have come from the Morris circle [85, 86]. Francesco Nonni, another xylographer associated with "Eroica," shows strong English affinities in such cuts as his "Euridiche," "Vere," and particularly in "Il Pino," [87] which shows certain linear conventions, reminiscent of Sturge Moore. Antonio Moroni shares the same "Ideen Kreis." Ettore di Giorgio's white line cutting of "The Annunication" [88] seems to show the Italian Renaissance influence after its passage through England. Our point, however, is not that these influences are real; even if they had nothing to do with England the spirit that has created them is not independent : it leans on extrinsic association for support. A proof of this may be seen for example in a set of ornaments for a Russian magazine "Energhia," designed by Emilio Mantelli, evidently in an attempt to create in the Russian manner. Mantelli was a very versatile xylographer who cultivated many different styles.

[1] An intellectual emotion is sometimes an aesthetic emotion at one or two removes.

From Ettore di Giorgio's woodcut: "The Annunciation." 7 × 5 in.   [88]

In the same way in which Mantelli designed his cuts when occasion demanded in an archaistically Russian style, Jean Lebedeff, a Russian, living in Paris, adapts his manner to whatever style the text may require. So he has illustrated a "King Lear" and a "Hamlet," "The Stories of Poushkine" and "A Life of the Martyrs" by Georges Duhamel, in varying stylistic conventions. On the others hand, he also cuts still-life and views in the modern manner. His convention is, nevertheless, fundamentally graphic, and his style, at least in the aforementioned book illustrations, associative rather than freely creative. Louis Jou, a Spaniard living in Paris, O. Eeckmann and Anthony de Witt, both Netherlanders, have all done, in the Flemish manner, excellent archaistic work.

The same also applies to the work of a Polish artist living in Warsaw, Wladislaw Skoczylas, only that he, instead of the black line, employs often after the manner of the Renaissance Italian Scolari, the white line. Skoczylas, an excellent draughtsman, has executed ten independent woodcuts on the subject of the Polish "Robin Hood" called Janosik.[1] [89] They are full of what will be recognized as the "Polish National Spirit." It may or may not be a genuine expression of "National" art, it is any way done very ably. We, however, get Skoczylas' real metal in a fine head of a Polish peasant [90], which is modelled with great force and engraved with consummate skill.

Skoczylas, the Pole, is in his technique as conservative as the Italian, Gino Barbieri, of whose virile work "Eroica" gives many examples ; it is only the subject matter that makes such things "modern."

More really national are cuts by Sonia Levitzka, who lives in Paris. They too, are either delicately archaic or naturalistic, but done entirely with the knife on soft wood. She is less interesting in her archaic illustrations than in her capital illustrations for Gogol's "Les Veillées du Hameau" [91]. Other books illustrated by her include "Les Coffres des Joyaux" and "Le Livre des Saintes paroles et des bons faits de notre Saint Roi Louis."

This artist, however, by reason of her pictorial and expressionistic qualities (she experiments with "portmanteau" cuts symbolizing complete union of two or more figures), hardly belongs to the category we have been reviewing here, who are distinguished by traditional and associative discipline of the elements of their design.

We, will, therefore, in the next chapter, consider work that is based on other principles than linear conventions and literary association.

[1] Dix bois originaux et inédits dessinés et gravés par W. S. Warsaw, 1920.

From J. E. Laboureur's woodcut decoration for " *Deux Dialogues des Dieux de Lucien.*" 2⅜ × 5½ in. [83]

THE EIGHTH CHAPTER: THE PICTORIAL DESIGN IN WHICH THE LITERARY ASSOCIATION IS SUBORDINATE

A T first sight, impressionism would seem an impossible theory to apply to a medium that deals so clearly with lines and so decisively with black and white only. Impressionism produced " form " only by manipulation of light values : it eschewed line, it abhorred sharp edges. England was, as regards drawing—from Rowlandson to Beardsley at all events—the home of the calligraphic contour ; France that of classic and impressionistic draughtsmanship. This may account for the fact that the impressionistic kind of woodcut which flourished, and still flourishes to some extent, further East on the Continent, has few representatives in England. French, German and Austrian, Dutch and Scandinavian artists developed a style of cutting which either gave in black and white *masses* the effect of something like bright sunlight, or they introduced atmospheric half-tone effects by means of additional flat-colour blocks in the Japanese method.

Much of this work of the first decade of this century, clever as it was, lacks to our modern eye both cohesion and interest. It would, however, not be fair to overlook here the claims of recognition of German artists like the veteran Wilhelm Laage, A. Haueisen, P. Dahlen,

119

From a woodcut by L. H. Bradshaw. 10 × 8 in. [88B]

H. Schroedter, Hans Frank, Karl Brendel, Karl Moll, and in particular Walter Klemm, of whom we shall have occasion to speak again. In England, naturalistic work has not developed along such lines, though in almost every other country this semi-impressionistic woodcut has its representation. What after all divides the artists of to-day more than frontiers is the manner in which they represent natural forms and accordingly we will deal here with those artists first who, though unfettered by linear convention, yet regard nature primarily, if not as a task-mistress, at all events as " she who must be obeyed " ; whilst those to whom nature is an impersonal storehouse or treasury from which forms and colours may be legitimately abstracted, shall be dealt with in the next chapter.

Amongst the foremost living artists, and in certain respects perhaps the foremost, is Frank Brangwyn, who has taken up the woodcut only since the beginning of the great war, when a serious illness kept him

120

From Wladislaw Skoczylas' woodcut for " Janosik." 6 × 7¼ in.

From a woodcut by Sonia Levitzka for Gogol's " Veillées du Hameau." 2 × 2 in.　　　　　　[91]

from doing the more physically strenuous work that has made his name famous in both hemispheres. Reckoned by his years, Brangwyn belongs to the older generation and to that sphere of influence to which both Gordon Craig and Nicholson belong—the concatenation is *via* James Pryde and Melville. The affinities express themselves neither in subject nor in technique, but in certain similarities of composition and boldness. Brangwyn informs me that he did a considerable amount of *wood engraving* in the orthodox manner in his early days, but I have seen no examples of it and so cannot judge of its qualities. Certain it is that his later cutting has no relation whatever with orthodox work or with that of the artists just mentioned. His style in his best and most characteristic cuts is a short nervous stabbing of the wood with the graver, almost analogous to the short stabbing touches of his brush on the huge canvases which carry his mural paintings. It is a style which is entirely his own. The design is in white line, roughly indicated, before the cutting, with chalk, but almost completely drawn in the cutting itself. His finest cut in this style is the " Via Dolorosa " [92], a sort of " J'accuse " inspired by Brangwyn's general outlook upon life, and the " Fair Wind " [93] printed in the now defunct " Form " and also, but exceedingly badly,[1] in that otherwise noble Italian effort " L'Eroica," the pioneer magazine of the Italian woodcut, which we have already referred to more than once. Another good woodcut showing Brangwyn's *glyptic* style is " The Exodus," printed in Mr. Shaw Sparrow's " Prints and Drawings by Frank Brangwyn " Of his smaller work the eight full page cuts for the Poems by Verhaeren, published by Pelletan Helleu, of Paris, are done in a, for him, unusually delicate manner. The " Modern Woodcutter " series contains several excellent examples, sometimes like " Sheep Shearing " [94] and " The Harvest," insignificant in dimension, but replete with meaning. Unfortunately, Brangwyn is far from pedantic in the handling of his own reputation. Cuts associated with his name are not always cut by him, and occasionally he will get an engraver to put in

[1] The Collector may find occasionally good signed proofs of many of Brangwyn's cuts, but they were never formally published or recorded.

122

From Wladislaw Skoczylas' woodcut : " Polish Peasant." $8\frac{1}{2} \times 8\frac{3}{8}$ in.

From a woodcut by Frank Brangwyn : "Sheep Shearing."
3 × 3¼ in.   [94]

a tone on a block that is otherwise of his own cutting, as in the
Verhaeren book ; the illustrations for a book on "Belgium," published
by Kegan Paul, were cut in wood very ably by H. G. Webb and
C. W. Moore. Without much trouble a little experience will, however,
enable one to distinguish between Brangwyn's best work and the
numerous other cuts—generally in facsimile of brush drawings—
which, even when cut by him are rarely so good or so important as
those I have singled out. Brangwyn's temperament is entirely opposed
to craftsmanship as an end in itself : he is, consequently, the despair
of minds who can only respond to materially demonstrable facts such
as those represented by orthodox methods of engraving and printing :
to him, therefore, the woodcut is sometimes a personal means of
expression, in which case it is instinct with the qualities of *carved*
wood ; but at other times it is to him merely a means of reproducing
a drawing which he will as lief hand over to a professional wood—or
even process—engraver. That in his personal and best work the result
should be of unrivalled excellence is due solely to the fact that he,
unlike most present-day artists, is a *natural* craftsman, whilst precisely
the most interesting work of the younger generation tends to be too
" sicklied o'er with the pale cast of thought." His approach to the
woodcut is, however, that of the painter ; hence on the one hand the
method of cutting white on black, on the other hand of using an

124

From the woodcut by Frank Brangwyn, R.A.: "Via Dolorosa." $7\frac{1}{2} \times 15$ in.

From a woodcut by Frank Brangwyn, R.A. : "A Fair Wind." $7\frac{1}{2} \times 12\frac{1}{2}$ in. [93]

infinite number of excisions which assume significance only in the aggregate.

This kind of cutting must not be confused with the lavishness of incision on which the tone engraver's technique is based ; nor does it bear any resemblance to Sturge Moore's manipulation of the tools, which is more subtle, if less masterful, than Brangwyn's. Brangwyn's cutting is wood *carving*, and is more closely related to the attitude of the sculptor than to that of the line draughtsman. His position as a xylographic artist is, therefore, nearer to Gauguin's, who was also a carver of wood, and of Munch's than to the work of their orthodox opponents. That this should be so is not so strange as might seem, seeing that the impressionist Brangwyn began—with his "Buccaneers" of 1893—to rebel against the same doctrines that drove the impressionist Frenchman and the impressionist Norwegian into other methods of opposition.

Greatly influenced by his admiration for Brangwyn's art is the work of his assistant, L. H. Bradshaw [88B], and also of the Belgian, R. A. Masui Castrique. Masui Castrique published here in London a series of fifty-five large size woodcuts illustrating " La Légende de Thyl Uylenspiegel." The cutting is done with considerable *verve*

125

From a woodcut by Gwendolen Raverat: "Sir Thomas Browne."
3½ × 4 in.   [95]

and the designs show a curious combination of Brangwynisms and Flemish "taste." But the influence of the English artist is in this case, as in most others known to me, baneful. Brangwyn is a powerful *natural* force, whose aesthetic intuition, rather than intellectual control, protects his creative instincts from disaster. Less forceful talents who copy his manner and mannerisms fail precisely to that extent : his " clothes " are too big for them, and hinder their freedom of movement. Masui Castrique's design is constantly tripped up by a conflict between the black line of the pen and the black mass of the brushtechnique, so that one often misses the significance of his considerable literary imagination.

Since we have touched upon Thyl Uylenspiegel and Belgian art, the work of another Belgian, Albert Jean Delstanche, may here be noted. Delstanche has published [1] a series of illustrations for Charles de Coster's " Tyl Ulenspiegel " and " The little Towns of Flanders." In both cases I find the drawings sound and interesting in a traditional sense and the cutting is highly expert, but from our point of

[1] Chatto & Windus.

126

From a woodcut by Gwendolen Raverat : " The Duck Pond."   4½ × 4 in.
[96]

view, without relevance, since it is almost entirely reproductive in the sense of the " facsimile cut."

Linked partly with the old reproductive line engraver's attitude towards the craft, partly with certain modern theories of design, is the work of one of the very best English xylographers, Gwendolen Raverat.

Mrs. Raverat, the wife of Jacques Raverat, the French painter, and daughter of Sir George Darwin, is an intensely English artist. I do not think that the merit of her work can be fully realized by anyone who is not intimately acquainted with English thought and feeling. The English character is proverbially reserved, and although a lot of nonsense is talked about the Englishman's lack of sentimentality, there is this foundation for such views that the English compared with most other peoples are not demonstrative; which, applied to Mrs. Raverat, simply means that there is a good deal more in her work than is apparent on the surface.

Gwendolen Raverat began to use the wood block for the purpose of giving expression to her aesthetic sense some eighteen years ago, and one of her first cuts, " The Knight of the Burning Pestle," is a piece of wood chopping such as one would expect from a talented English boy : it is cut on soft wood with a knife. " The Cobbled Yard," another early woodcut, leaves no doubt as to the femininity of its author, but it has masculine independence of expression, and a clearly indicated will to obtain a perfect control over her medium. This control the artist has achieved, and it is this which makes her merit unusual as a woman's and outstanding as an artist's. At first she was attracted by figure subjects, usually with an associative meaning, as, for instance, in " The Quarrel " and in the excellent white line cut " The Gypsies," where the preponderance of the black masses is naturally accounted for as a light value, the scene being a camp fire by night time. Here her unusual strength is shown, however, not by the ancient *tour de force* of lighting, but by the capital execution of details, such as the drawing of hands and feet and the treatment of drapery. Similarly excellent and characteristic is her little illustration for the " Ballad of Clerk Saunders." In the year 1912 she comes under the influence of Eric Gill, and in such subjects as " The Visitation," " The Creation of Light " and the " Piétà," of which she painted a large version in oil, her treatment becomes somewhat affected and Byzantine. The engraved line is less obviously " woody," but for that reason an excellent disciplinary exercise for the cutter's hand. Mrs. Raverat has engraved a large number of figure subjects, using the white line on

128

From a woodcut by Gwendolen Raverat: " David, Old " (Abishag the Shunammite).
5½ × 4¼ in.   [97]

From a woodcut by E. M. Darwin: "The Bath." 3 × 2½ in.   [98]

hard wood with great skill ("The Nativity," "Margaret's Ghost"), with fine imagination ("Sir Thomas Browne," the "neighbour unto the grave" [95]) and without the affectation of Byzantinisms. Some of the most remarkable work is, however, a series of landscapes which at first sight remind one of the style of the professional wood engravers of the seventies or eighties. It is here, however, that her English reserve shows itself. The subjects themselves are entirely commonplace; there is no *romantic* frippery and trimming; no "beautiful" scenery. Here are some of her titles: "The Edge of the Wood," "Autumn Morning," "November Day," "Full Moon," "Poplars in France." The titles are just and entirely indicative of the subjects, but it is the skill with which the artist has expressed the sentiment that causes admiration. The blocks are for the most part quite diminutive, scarcely exceeding four or five square inches, but the amount of emotional values she manages to express within this narrow compass is truly remarkable. In a little block called "The Moor" there is enough matter to fill a page of descriptive writing. These little engraved blocks are things that depend entirely on themselves, they are not decorations for a book page; in fact they have none of those qualities which are called decorative. This is perhaps the reason that the artist has exchanged this method of engraving

130

From a woodcut by J. F. Greenwood : " John Atherton's Mill."
5 × 4 in.   [99]

landscapes for another in which the incisions are not nearly so fine and so numerous; indeed, bold silhouetting of black masses gives a quality which is at once more decorative, more luminous and more obviously "woody" (*e. g.*, "Sheep by a River," "The Duck Pond" [96]).

Amongst the latest cuts are bold soft wood blocks of still more decorative nature ("The Bathers," "Boys Dancing"), but these are not perhaps as successful as her earlier figure and landscape engravings on hard wood, nor as her more recent blocks partly on soft wood ("The Mountain Road," "The Bridge"), partly on hard wood ("David, Old" [97] and "Le Jeu de Boules" and the "Bowl Players," in which latter she has realized a more forceful expression of three-dimensional composition).

I have dwelt at some length on this artist's cuts, not only because it is so entirely sound technically and sane mentally, yielding its beauty nevertheless only to the sensitive, but because in Gwendolen Raverat's work intellectual values hold a careful balance to the emotional elements : it thus becomes in its different phases a useful indicator of the various lines along which modern xylographers have developed their medium.

In Mrs. Raverat's technique there are examples of the bold primitive

131

From a woodcut by J. F. Greenwood : " Cove Lane."

From a woodcut by Stephen Bone. Original size.   [101]

cut ("The Knight of the Burning Pestle"), of the line engraver's art
("King Lear"), of the pictorial cut in bold masses ("Gypsies"), of
bold white line design ("Child Stealers"), of fine black line ("The
Prodigal") and coarse black line ("Boys Dancing"), of sheer
orthodox engraving ("Le Pelvoux"), of nervous pictorial white line
("The Bridge," "Street by Moonlight"), of purely associative composition ("The Nightingale"), so that acquaintance with her work
enables the beginner to obtain the right focus when examining other
manifestations of modern xylographic aims and conceptions.
The work of Mrs. Raverat's sister-in-law should here not be passed
over without notice. Mrs. Darwin first instructed her in the use of
the tools and there are certain affinities in the treatment of subject
matter which clearly show the influence of her teaching. Mrs.
Darwin's "Sister and Brother" is decorative in a pleasant and very
simple manner and "The Bath" [98] well designed and well cut.
In certain respects akin to Mrs. Raverat's landscape engraving, in
others nearer Sydney Lee's manner of handling the material, is the

133

From a woodcut by J. J. Lankes: "Winter." 4 × 6 in. [102]

work of J. F. Greenwood. Greenwood uses exclusively the white line. His views of his native Yorkshire are cut not only with a firm feeling for "local colour" but also with a good sense of composition. Of his engravings, "The Dale Road," "Cove Lane" [100] and "The Tinker," as well as the imaginative "Richmond," are amongst the best things he has so far engraved, though his slightly sentimental, but quite imaginative "Poplars" and "John Atherton's Mill" [99] appeal perhaps to a wider public.

Good naturalistic work is done particularly in this country. We can here only single out Noel and P. Kerr Rooke, Millicent Jackson, Margaret Pilkington, C. A. Wilkinson, G. Soper and W. E. Robins; the technique of the two latter, however, is a proof that they are more versed in a different medium, *viz.*, etching. Muirhead Bone's young son, Stephen, also practises a very accomplished technique of engraving [101] which is, nevertheless, more careful and often more elaborate than economical and striking, and not nearly so interesting as the comparative failures of his latest attempts at direct cutting.

134

From a woodcut by Tod Lindenmuth: "A Village Street." 16½ × 13 in. [103]

From a woodcut by C. O. Woodbury : One of the " Beeches of Burnham " Series.   8 ×7 in.   [105]

136

From a wood engraving by P. Rusicka: "Brooklyn Bridge." $7\frac{1}{2} \times 7$ in.

From a woodcut by Birger Sandzén. 8 × 6 in. [106]

Work of a related quality, aiming at *naturalistic* effect at a small expenditure of imagination is, for that reason, probably plentiful in all European countries. Representative craftsmen of this kind are, *e.g.*, in America, J. J. Lankes [102] and Tod Lindenmuth [103], whilst the veteran P. Rusicka's technique would link him rather with the wood engravers of the eighties but for the fact that such prints as his " Brooklyn Bridge " [104], reveal, apart from Japanese influences of composition, an independent and personal technique in the treatment of the water. Another American, C. O. Woodbury, also a hardwood engraver, interests from the point of view of content or subject matter. His tree studies, inspired, curiously enough, by our very English " Burnham Beeches " [105], are endowed with a personality which makes these hoary ancients appear like souls in purgatory. Unfortunately, Woodbury's technique, accomplished as it is, falls short in the matter both of design and of truly creative tooling.

138

From a woodcut by Gustave Zévort : " Le Pont des Arts, Paris." 5¼×7 in.   [107]

Care and elaboration of detail is, as one repeatedly experiences, not a quality that makes for creative expression. It, therefore, happens that work which is perhaps not of the highest order possesses, nevertheless, a greater interest. Such, for instance, is the case with the cuts by the American, Birger Sandzén [106], whose amusing atmospheric formula for cutting, like the orthodox etching formula of his master Zorn, tends to become too mechanical. More varied are the formulæ for atmospheric effects practised by the Frenchman G. Zévort. Better work is done by the latter's compatriots, Paul Emile Pissarro, Chalandre, Rouquet, P. E. Colin and many others. Actually, however, Zévort's technique is more venturesome. The problem he seems to have set himself is that of the treatment of skies and clouds and the light effects for which they are responsible. He does not shrink from the employment of means that would appear to be the least likely. His technique is based on the pen line, that is to say,

139

From a woodcut by Gustave Zévort : " Dordrecht." 6 × 4 in. [108]

From a woodcut by Gustave Zévort : "Auxerre." 8 × 5½ in.

From a woodcut by Louis Moreau : " The River." [110]

its foundation is the black line, but whilst he keeps his execution of
the landscape both graphic and impressionistic, his treatment of
sky and cloud forms is unorthodox and at first thought unjustifiable.
Sometimes a few scrawls or parallels of "pen line" will suffice to
indicate cloud and sky [107]; at other times, the lines take the shape
of a black mesh [108]; at yet other times he resorts to the old
" manière criblée " [109] and dots his sky with a mass of regular white
spots. Often enough his experiment does not succeed ; but when, as
in the examples illustrated, it does succeed, the effect is both luminous
and more convincing than one would expect it to be.
Another French artist whose graphic experiments in the treatment of
sky, water and smoke effects are exceedingly interesting is Louis
Moreau, known to English readers through the reproductions of his
cuts in the magazine " Form." In a Riviera landscape, " Nice," he

142

From a woodcut by Jack Roberts: " La Rue du Calvaire."
13 × 5½ in.   [111]

143

From a linoleum cut by Henry Glintenkamp: One of the " Twelve Linoleum Cuts of Spain." 6¼ × 8¾ in.
[112]

has employed a hard and almost geometrical linear device with which he renders light effects in sky and water nevertheless in a manner that is convincing : it is the burning sky and the soft oily water of a Mediterranean evening. Even more interesting because anti-glyptic is a river landscape of his [110]. Here he has woven a wiry linear pattern out of water- and smoke-shapes which has little to do with wood as a medium, but is interesting for its own sake and curiously effective.

We have called this sort of thing anti-glyptic because it does violence to the natural use of the xylographic tools, or rather to the natural movement of the hand on the wood.

The reverse is true of a large number of modern wood and linoleum cuts in which the design is produced by the simplest strokes or pushes of the gouge, based on the methods of impressionistic brush work. Examples of this kind of soft wood cutting are plentiful in every country, except in England. Jack Roberts, an Englishman living in

144

From a woodcut by Emilio Mantelli : " Il Bevitore. "   9×7½ in.

From a woodcut by Dr. Emma Bormann : " The Gallery of the Opera House, Vienna." $5\frac{3}{4} \times 22\frac{3}{4}$ in. [113]

Paris, has done a series of views of Paris in this manner [111]. And quite recently an American, Henry Glintenkamp, has produced a series of Mexican and Spanish views [112] cut in this manner in linoleum. On the continent snow landscapes which present the artist with a "black and white" design, so to speak, "cut and dried," are frequent subjects for this kind of coarse cutting. The *snow* necessitates the removal of a great deal of wood surface and the accidental relief, cut by the tool in the wood and visible often in the impressed print, has given the artists opportunity to exploit the accidents. We mention amongst "cunning" snow cutters Karl Moll, in Germany, and Olaf Willums, in Norway. The latter manages to give his " snow " delicate half-tones which are actually merely the shadows cast by the raised surfaces of the print. In the Japanese " stone-prints " the " relief " which the medium almost invites is exploited with a different effect; the *whites* being raised above the black backgrounds.

Japanese methods of printing in flat maplike masses have inspired much of European xylography, sometimes with very pleasing results. I mention amongst the best of this kind, snow landscapes by the German, Fräulein von Frede, the Dane, H. C. Barenheldt, and the Swede, Else Bjorkman, the Belgian, André Carpantier, and so almost *ad infinitum*.

It is impossible here to do the subject justice ; each country seems to bring forth a sufficient number of artists capable of producing good *naturalistic* woodcuts with the help of two or more printings in colour : and their merit is the greater the less they resemble Japanese prints or European colour reproductions.

If Ingres said that the line is the probity of painting, so it should be understood that the black and white is the probity of the woodcut. It is this change from Ingres' line to the impressionistic drawing in planes which characterizes the modern manner. A transition may be

146

From a woodcut by Dr. Emma Bormann: " Scene-shifting." $18\frac{1}{2} \times 14\frac{1}{2}$ in.

studied to advantage in such a cut as Mantelli's "Il Bevitore" [112A]. It began manifestly as a drawing in Ingres' sense, *i.e.*, with black contour line and shading, as shown, *e.g.*, by the treatment of the face and the nose in particular. But as the artist was working with a coarse cutter, the lines were thick, the shading instead of being produced by black lines tended to become black planes; contour and shade lines interchange their functions—in the bottle it is difficult to say whether the contour is black or white; in the window frame one of the lines is a contour, the other is partly contour, partly shadow plane losing itself in the colour value of the landscape background, where again a roof and three windows are outlined in white, which thus ceases to be a light value. One could continue to analyse this point and to show how black and white, instead of being as in Ingres' and all academic art a strictly rigid and immutable convention, have, in the modern artists' handling, a protean variety of functions and tending to disappear into planes (compare, for example, especially many portrait cuts in the manner of Vallotton, such as have been done by Baudier and Gallien [144], in France, Sahlèn in Sweden, Hummel, Wurttemberger in Germany, and many others).

It is this that makes the naturalistic subjects of the Austrian xylographer, Dr. Emma Bormann, so admirable. This artist delights in rendering townscapes, interiors of theatres and concert rooms, or little incidents in the life of her stricken city, Vienna. She works with the grain on soft wood or linoleum white on black with short nervous digs which render *lines* only by a succession of white dots. The method of drawing is manifestly based on impressionist principles, her black and white being always used as light and tone values, the colour often being added, sparingly, by hand. One of the best cuts is a view of the Vienna Opera House [113], in which the countering of whites and blacks produces not only *tone*, but also a delightful sparkle of light. In another, and technically more audacious print, "Szenen Umbau" [114], the artist has attempted a broader manner of cutting than generally characterizes her composition. A woodcut of hers: "the Funeral of the murdered socialist, Dr. Kautsky, in Munich," is printed with an additional tone block. The print is somewhat confused, probably intentionally so, for the confusion, together with the angry acute angles of the red flags which pierce the surface at many points, adds psychologically to the truth of the subject.

Dr. Bormann excels, indeed, not only in the handling of crowds, as the Circus scene here reproduced [115] may help to prove, she

148

From a woodcut by Dr. Emma Bormann: " Piazza at Trau." 23 × 16¼ in.

[116]

From a woodcut by Dr. Emma Bormann: "Circus." 13½ × 16 in.   [115]

handles even architectural details in a cleverly synthetic manner [116]
which makes one overlook the absence of the Architect's " stand-by,"
the ruler-drawn line. The treatment of the sky in the view of Trau
should be compared with Zévort's [107, 108, 109].
There is on the surface no connection between Dr. Bormann's method
of cutting and that of the French illustrator, Hermann Paul. Nevertheless, Hermann Paul's striking manner is, like the Viennese artist's,
directly due to impressionistic realism. The greatest difference between
the two is the nature of the incision, or rather excision—but with both
black and white are mainly light values, though the Frenchman uses
them quite definitely for decorative purposes. His manner of handling
black is, strictly speaking, not suitable for book illustration, nor has it
the usual French or classic elegance. He is, as a matter of fact, a pure
150

From a woodcut by Hermann Paul : One of the " Danse Macabre " Series. 4½ × 5 in.
[117]

Gothic, as the choice of works illustrated by him proves. There are the twenty compositions for " Le Doctrinal des Preux " ; a " Danse Macabre "[117]; the " Chansons de France," and above all, the outstanding congruousness of his Rabelais illustrations [118]. Hermann Paul has humour in the composition and wit in the cutting. Nothing is done that the simple tool cannot conveniently do, and it is astonishing what it *can* do in his hand : the design is exclusively the tool's and not the pen's or the pencil's.

If we compare with the excellent Hermann Paul the accomplished work of the Spaniard, Louis Jou, we notice at once the difference between the former artist, who thinks in the terms of his medium, and the latter, who thinks in the terms of another. Both of them are, so far as representation goes, naturalistic, but whereas Hermann Paul's xylographic manner is the result of drawing with the tool, Jou's is the result of making the tool translate a picture into a preconceived

151

From a woodcut by Hermann Paul : One of the illustrations for Rabelais' "Gargantua." 6 × 4¼ in. [118]

formula of xylography. Jou's technique is much more complicated, and though perfectly legitimate, less spontaneous, as his series of religious subjects done in the "gothic" manner and with chiaroscuro tone bear out. He has, however, one—in xylography—excessively rare quality, he gets the effect of full *colour* into his black and white [119] to a greater extent than almost any artist hitherto considered.

A woodcutter whose cutting is not divorced from the designing by one remove, and who, therefore, resembles Hermann Paul rather than Louis Jou in technique, is the Dutchman, L. O. Wenckebach. This artist has a distinguished series of independent woodcuts to his credit, in which he has arranged his design in broad black and white masses without half-tones on the impressionistic (light value) principle. His themes are usually taken from popular legend (Tyll Uylenspiegel) or the Bible. Nothing could be better than his versions of " The Good Samaritan," particularly the one in which the ass is shown with its head raised [120]. There are many other subjects done in the simplest

152

From a woodcut by Louis Jou: "Portrait of a Poet."   14×10 in.   [119]

From a woodcut by L. O. Wenckebach : "The Good Samaritan."   8½×7 in.

From a woodcut by L. O. Wenckebach : " Christ driving out the Money Changers." $11\frac{3}{4} \times 9$ in.   [121]

From a woodcut by Walter Klemm: "Peasants of Dachau leaving Church." 9¾ × 10 in. [122]

black and white manner, but most striking is perhaps his " Christ driving the money changers out of the Temple " [121]. Here the dominating figure of Christ expels the offenders by a gesture which translates itself aesthetically into lines of tremendous centrifugal force. Compared with Wenckebach's handling of the tool, that of Walter Klemm, Germany's best naturalistic xylographer, whom we have already mentioned, is more accomplished. Beginning with highly finished and extremely competent realistic subjects, Klemm's design gradually broadened out into black and white impressionism [122], not

156

From a woodcut by Walter Klemm : One of the illustrations for " Don Quixote." $9\frac{3}{4} \times 8\frac{3}{4}$ in.   [123]

From a woodcut by Walter Klemm. One of the illustrations for
Flaubert's " St. Julien." 5½ × 3½ in. [124]

unlike Dr. Bormann's in treatment. His portfolio of " Don Quixote "
illustrations contains brilliant examples of direct designing in wood.
In the earlier work there was much representational accuracy, great
skill, and in certain cuts imagination in the literary sense, but the
light and colour values fought each other in black and white. In the
" Don Quixote " illustrations Klemm has definitely accepted black
and white as light values and he handles his tools with an extraordinary
economy, force and subtlety. His " Don Quixote " illustrations are
pure forceful realism without any " decorative " trimming [123]. The

158

From a woodcut by Jean Marchand: from "L'Almanach du Citronier."
3 × 4½ in. [125]

variety of expression, the subtlety of simplification and the luminosity
of his black and white are wholely admirable.

The apparent modernism of Klemm's illustrations for Flaubert's
" St. Julien l'Hospitallier " [124] is explained by the artist as an
attempted archaicism. One cannot, however, help feeling that so stern
a naturalist and realist would not have ventured so far without the
ubiquitous influence of more advanced theories. Compare for style
of cutting the modernist's Jean Marchand's cut [125].

A different temperament, a different technique and inasmuch as the
purpose is changed from the single independent print to the illustration
for the printed page, is shown in the work of Gabriel Daragnès, the
French xylographer whom we mention at the end of this chapter
because his work presents a sort of resumé of the possibilities in a
method of design that is willing to adopt any means of expression
compatible with adherence to naturalistic representation, whether in
linear or mass composition, whether white on black or black on white.
Daragnès has illustrated Oscar Wilde's " Ballad of Reading Gaol ";
Gerard de Nerval's " Main Enchantée "; Goethe's " Faust." He is,
I think, seen at his best in a series of illustrations for Paul Claudel's
" Protée." He shows here a sense of colour as well as beautiful drafts-
manship in execution; he has humour and invention and an elegance

159

which makes Klemm's cutting look unpolished [126, 127]. The opposite illustration is the headpiece to Act II. of "Protée": "Le Satyre Majeur à l'orchestra":

> " *Tout beaux Messieurs, tout doux*
> *Plus bas, plus bas.* . . . . "

But in such illustrations as his frontispiece to " Le Corbeau," Poe's "Raven," we see that he too, like the Laboureur, is forsaking simple naturalism in favour of post-impressionistic—using the word in its chronological sense—composition.

From a woodcut tailpiece by Daragnès [See 126]. 3¼ × 5¼ in.   [127]

From a woodcut by Daragnès: One of the illustrations for Claudels' "Protée"
(Le Satyre Majeur). 4¾ × 5 in. [126]

161

From a woodcut by J. E. Laboureur: "Au Luxembourg," 1897.   [127B]

THE NINTH CHAPTER: A SHORT ONE, PREPARING THE GROUND FOR THE CHANGE THAT HAS COME OVER THE ARTIST'S ATTITUDE TOWARDS NATURE

WENTY-FIVE years ago, Laboureur, whose woodcuts now belong entirely to the modern movement in art, was already seen to struggle with the problem of combining impressionistic light values with a firm decorative composition. His print of the Luxembourg Gardens [127B], published in "L'Image," showed ostensibly only a couple of "bonnes" with their charges in the famous gardens. The technique was a strong coarse black and white, suggesting sunlight in a loose impressionistic manner ; but the play he made with the round children's hats, and the caps and ribbons of the nurses, in contrast to the confused mass of the trees, shows clearly how conscious he was of the necessity of aesthetic *structure* in design. A decorative border pattern, in the same number, made up of abstract pattern—not traditional ornament—gives further proof of his early searching for more purely aesthetic values.

It is with the growth of the new conception of design out of impressionism that we are more especially here concerned ; and for this purpose the work of the Venetian Guido Marussig, furnishes particularly useful material. Marussig published in the "Eroica," of 1912, a woodcut entitled : " Pali striati e ippocastani fioriti "—" Striped poles and blooming horse chestnut " [128]. The subject was taken from a common Venetian sight, but what interested the artist was the *colour* pattern made by the poles and the " candles " of the chestnut trees. In another very similar cut, " Palazzi illuminati," the blacks and whites are partly light and partly colour values, but the effect in both cases is that of a flat black and white colour pattern.

In England, Robert Gibbings has taken this kind of naturalistic pattern weaving a step further. He began by purely naturalistic landscape designing with *white* lines, but the war took him to the South and the East, and the cubic Oriental houses impelled him to build up cubic patterns in black and white in which these two " colours " function not only as colour and lights but also as distinctly plastic, *i.e.*, three dimensional values [129]. One can see by comparison of Gibbings' with Marussig's manner how much less sentimental and

From a woodcut by Guido Marussig: "Striped poles and blooming horse chestnut."
5½ × 5½ in.

[128]

more intellectual impressionism had become. Impressionism, however, it still is *au fond*, for when we see Gibbings applying his method to slightly different subjects, such as " Dublin in Snow," or " Cornwall," the so-called " cubism " resolves itself into a pattern of shadows and lights without contours or half-tones. The artist next essayed the same method with the human figure seen undraped against a bare rock of the sea-shore. The darks or blacks of this cut represent the shadows, the lights, contourless and mostly undefined, are the blank spaces of the paper. There is a conflict between the light and colour values which, coupled with the naturalistic foundation of the design, detracts

164

From a woodcut by Robert Gibbings : " Melleha, Malta." 7½ × 7½ in.

From a woodcut by C. W. R. Nevinson: "Lorry Jumpers." 8½ × 11¼ in. [131]

from its success. In his portrait of William Walcot [130], Gibbings' method, helped by the dark masses of hair, beard and clothes, and the absence of a difficult background, shows itself to greater advantage. Somewhat similar means have been employed by C. W. R. Nevinson in the cut here illustrated [131]; though the design has been influenced by the artist's cubistic studies—Nevinson is one of our pre-war "Futurist" revolutionaries—the composition is, nevertheless, so realistic that an underexposed snapshot might have served as its foundation. Xylographically, Nevinson's cutting shows greater regard for the medium than Gibbings', whose sharp edges suggest, if anything, scissor designed black paper silhouettes. Gibbings, however, loves definiteness, *i.e.*, a sweeping clear-cut contour for its own sake. It will be seen then, that designs like Nevinson's and Gibbings', however simplified and "abstract" in appearance, are fundamentally representational and naturalistic, but their disciplining of contours shows the drift away from nature as a task mistress.

166

From a woodcut by Alberto Caligiani : One of the " Visioni di Montagnana."   6¼ × 6¼ in.   [133]

167

From a woodcut by Robert Gibbings : " Portrait of William Walcot." $11\frac{3}{4} \times 5\frac{1}{4}$ in.   [130]

From a woodcut by Edward Wadsworth: "Minesweepers." 2 × 5⅜ in. [137]

THE TENTH CHAPTER: FREE AND CREATIVE DESIGN AND THE DRIFT AWAY FROM IMITATION OF NATURE

IF there is a definite parting of the ways between the old and the new orientation in art it may be recognized—superficially—by a modification of "drawing," which goes, as pointed out, beyond mere elimination or elaboration of detail or correction and "improvement" of natural form and approaches often the *distorted* and *unnatural*.

As repeatedly urged in these pages, the greater number of the public are still under the impression that the artist's principal task consists in painting or drawing things as they *are* and preferably "beautiful" things. Language being a very unreliable means of conveying thought with any degree of precision this greater number are completely mystified when they hear certain modern pictures which appear to them utterly unlike "nature" described as even more *real* than "old-fashioned" ones. It is said, for instance, that Cézanne aimed at the reality behind the appearance of

From a woodcut by Wassili Kandinsky. 4 × 4¾ in. [177]

From a woodcut by Gino Sensani: "The Dancers."
6¼ × 4¾ in.   [132]

things. This is, however, not strictly true : no human intellect can get at the reality of any object ; so that in that respect the conservatives and the revolutionaries are equally wide of their mark. The only *reality* we know is in ourselves and the Delphic " know thyself " still remains a counsel of perfection. All that artists have ever been able to do is to represent things, not as they *really* are, but as the artists see them. The whole meaning and mystery of art lies cradled in that one little conception: *seeing*—both as a mechanico-optical and a psycho-mental function. All modifications, deviations, distortions and abstractions of and from *nature* by art, incompetence excepted, are due to different ways of *seeing*.

That the artist of whatever school, epoch or environment of necessity *always* modifies the data of nature in his design would be more obvious than it is if mankind relied only on the message which the outer eye receives and conveys to the inner mental nerve centre objectively. The " image," however, which reaches this centre is instantly received

170

From a woodcut by Charles Ginner: "A Cornish Cottage." Original size.

[134]

by ever alert " associations " which crowd around it like a throng of touts and traders round a ship arriving in an Oriental port. What finally happens to the image when it has *landed* will depend ultimately on the persuasive power of aforesaid associations and the nature of the individuals " bent," or in Freudian terminology, " complex."

So long as the individual artist creates, not, to be sure, in accordance with his optic vision, but in obedience to expectant associations, and so long as these associations are shared by the majority of his public, no difficulty arises, and his expression, his message, is understood by all. A change of associations or a different direction taken by them owing to some new cause will bring about a change in conceptions, which in art means a change in style.

The differences that make the change in the design of to-day are, there-fore, due to a change of associations which the artists have made, but which the public do not—as yet—generally share. The modern artist has learnt to look upon the work of art as an autonomous thing which must obey the laws of art rather than the laws of outside "nature." It is of course not independent of life, or nature, but a manifestation of both. This autonomy of art, involving as it does a deviation from " nature " and, therefore, causing the present-day public so much difficulty has, nevertheless, long been accepted by them, not only without a murmur of disapproval, but on the contrary with the greatest appreciation, Traditional ornament, for example, is always a modification and dis-tortion of " nature " unless it is an altogether unnatural, *i.e.*, a geomet-rical device ; and caricature is still the delight of the broadest strata of the public. It will be seen, therefore, that even the most hide-bound are willing to accept wildly improbable representations of " nature " without demur and even with applause, provided their perception is accompanied by suitable associations.

Now caricature is a perfectly rational and legitimate approach to the tendencies of modern art. Caricature, if it has any claim to art at all, is a design *loaded* [1] with an excess of meaning, of character. It *over*-emphasizes the appearance of things—generally human beings—and invests them with a truth that would otherwise be concealed behind the surface ; so much so, that a good caricature is more *like* a person than a photograph, to say nothing of paintings of the common order.

It is clear, therefore, that an artist may load his design in accordance with the particular character he wishes to stress. The amusing wood-cuts of the Italian, Gino Sensani—another of the artists associated with

Caricature : from caricare, *to load*.

172

From a woodcut by Charles Ginner: "Dieppe."   12 × 10 in.

the magazine " Eroica "—will, in all probability, be accepted as almost normal if " *un po ricercate e volute* " designs verging on caricature perhaps, but not unnatural [132]. So likewise the work of one of his colleagues, Alberto Caligiani, would be accepted as good examples of direct woodcutting with an intentional caricature inflection. Whilst, however, no one would accuse Guido Marussig or Robert Gibbings of having caricatured their representations of Italian, Greek or Maltese cities, Caligiani's "Visioni di Montagnana " [133] are in the nature of caricatures ; the exaggerations and even distortions are here due to a literary and sentimental conception of art which seeks for the *human* relation, for human moods in the landscape.

A comparison of Charles Ginner's woodcuts with these proves that he has a very different conception of art and one that many misunderstand [134, 135]. In Ginner's cuts the design is loaded in respect of flat pattern : they are fine vertical compositions with no illusion of depth ; they have the quality of an embroidery, a lace-like patterning, that has no sentimental associations and in their hand-coloured form are seen to be purely flat decorations.

If we now look at a design in three colours by Edward Wadsworth, and learn that it represents a Greek town, " Riponelli," we conclude that the design is *loaded* cubically [136]. That is to say, the artist, dismissing all sentimental associations from his mind, has used the cubic aspect of the church and houses of this town in order to produce a cubic " in and out " pattern intended to entertain the eye. In other woodcuts of this artist—the earlier ones as a matter of fact, such as " In dry dock " and " Minesweepers " [137]—there is no actual distortion ; they are flat, but as realistic as Gibbings', the difference being that Wadsworth selected his natural facts and has built up his design, not on the data of external nature, but on the internal problem of design : in other words, in Gibbings' case the advancing and receding lines, the black and white shapes are selected on a representational schedule : in Wadsworth's case the same elements come up for selection for their own sakes, that is : *because* they are capable of being shaped into black and white patterns ; if they also happen to signify actual things, such as ships, funnels, docks, that is merely incidental, but not essential. A further step is taken by Wadsworth in his view of " Tarmacs" [138]. In this cut, which has for its subject a Black Country " slagheap," geometrical has given way to emotional abstraction ; the landscape is seen not so much as what it *looks* like, but as what it *feels* like. How closely, nevertheless, natural and

174

From Edward Wadsworth's woodcut in three colours :
" Riponelli."   Slightly reduced.   [136]

From a woodcut by Edward Wadsworth: "Tarmacs." 5¾ × 4 in.   [138]

aesthetic selection, that is, optic sight and aesthetic feeling, are mutually related a comparison of this cut with a more freely representative rendering of the "Ravin de la Caillette," a chiaroscuro print by Henri Marret, reproduced in the "Studio" special number, will show : it would take very little to convert this picture of another kind of slagheap into a Wadsworthian conception. Amongst the fourteen woodcuts of Wadsworth's, published in the "Modern Woodcutter" series, there is a still-life composition with a cactus for its principal rhythm [139] ; in such designs quite as much as in his landscapes "he depends," to quote from Mr. Arnold Bennett's preface to the Artists' Black Country Exhibition Catalogue, "on his central vitalizing emotion, and he allows no extrinsic facts (which facts none knows more intimately than he) to interfere with the expression of the emotion. His courage in this respect may disconcert the timid. And a good thing too ! " Though the " Five Town novelist's " emotional exclamation seems a little out of place in connection with so simple a matter as the disconcerting of the already timid he is justified in laying stress on the fact

175

From a woodcut by Edward Wadsworth : "Cactus." 6 × 4 in.   [139]

that " extrinsic facts," or what we would call associative ideas, are not the criteria of aesthetic achievement, which depends on the shapes rather than the content of things. In reference to our still-life subject this means that Wadsworth has, unlike Disertori, the Italian artist, whose window motif is here reproduced [140], no sentimental attachment to the plant, the window or the table, but only to the rhythmic pattern of black and white he can build up with the aid of such " extrinsic facts " into a picture with a composition in a vertical (two

176

From a woodcut by Benvenuto Disertori : " Still life."   5½ × 5½ in.   [140]

dimensional) and horizontal (three dimensional) sense. This still life clearly points to Wadsworth's artistic pedigree ; it is like most *modern* art of post-impressionistic complexion—of Parisian origin. I say advisedly Parisian, because it is not French in any national sense, being in fact, like most " modern " art, the result of international confluences which have their basin in Paris.

The principal innovation, so far as our western conception of design is concerned, caused by this Parisian " pool " is the conscious establishment of the picture-plane as an aesthetic reality—that is to say,

DD   **177**

From a woodcut by Vanessa Bell.   Illustration for " Kew Gardens."
6 ×4 in.   [142]

its destruction as the basis of an illusion of *nature*, real or pretended.
The lines and planes, the shapes of colour and the third-dimensional
illusion of depth are combined—as in Wadsworth's cactus picture—
into an organic whole, which must be judged as an aesthetic unit rather
than as a copy of representation of nature. Instead of regarding the
frame of a painting or the mount of a print as an opening into an
178

From a woodcut by E. McKnight Kauffer: " Flight." 5½ ×9 in.

illusion, these things become merely the delimitation or borders of an aesthetic design. The importance of the distinction lies in the fact that natural perspective, as well as representational accuracy and arbitrary standards of " beauty," have, in the " modern " conception of art, definitely ceased to be criteria of " truth."

According to this conception each artist determines his own lines and curves, *i.e.*, establishes his own standard for each work he creates, and so may legitimately be criticised only if he falls short of his own standard implied in his work. This means, in other words, that an artist who sets out for a realistic " copy " of nature may be judged on the basis of representational accuracy, whilst another whose object is the design of a decorative pattern, cannot be taken to task if he fails in *representational* accuracy, nor should a third one be derided if he make mincemeat of accuracy and hash of decoration, *provided he establishes some other definite order in his work of art*—which is in itself essentially order. This liberty throws at once greater responsibility on the artist and the necessity of collaboration on the spectator, a voluntary necessity, of course, since there can be no compulsion in the relationship of artist and public. The practice and the appreciation of art thus becomes a much more adventurous thing than

179

From a woodcut by A. P. Gallien : "Portrait of the Artist Zadkine."
Original size.   [144]

it used to be. If the " genius " of the artist stands or falls by his practice,
the judgment upon it stands or falls by the spectator's own capacity;
there is no other court.

It will be gathered from this that *modernity* in art depends not so
much on craftsmanship as such, but as a means of expressing the
design and intention of the artist. From the purely xylographic point
of view, however, neither Wadsworth nor other English artists' work
of similar tendencies stands very high because the material—the wood
—is not essential to its expression.

180

From one of " Twelve Woodcuts " by Roger Fry.   5½ × 4 in.   [141]

181

From a woodcut by A. P. Gallien: "Café Concert de l'Avenue du Maine." 3½ × 7½ in. [145]

Wadsworth is associated with the Wyndham Lewis group of intellectual artists, a group that is influenced by Picasso, and so forms a later development of the earlier Parisian school of post-impressionists, whose first apostle and missionary in England is Roger Fry. Roger Fry's art is sensible, in the old-fashioned sense of the word, rather than intellectual; his little book of " Twelve Woodcuts " seems to me unequal in merit ; but the cut here illustrated [141] is remarkable as a suggestion of three-dimensional composition. Other xylographers associated with his school are Duncan Grant, Claude Wolfe, Vanessa Bell, Roald Kristian—a Swede, and imitator of bushmen's or prehistoric mannerisms—and MacKnight Kauffer, an American-Londoner. There is a little cut of Vanessa Bell's entitled " Kew Gardens " [142], a coarse, black line cut which illustrates the tendency of a great deal of this kind of design to become picture puzzles. " Cherchez les femmes " would be a good title for this ostensibly horticultural cut, which is, nevertheless, a " promenade " of two ladies. The *puzzling* nature of this method of design is accounted for by the fact that the " vitalizing emotion " is not, as in traditional art, the content, but the data it supplies for the designer, who combines, in this case, horticultural and anthropological elements into an open though carefully constructed organization of forms. One could, nevertheless, point out traditionally designed cuts, such as several of Sturge Moore's —" Love in the Wood "—in which the " content " is perhaps even more puzzlingly concealed, because there is no obvious " pattern."

182

From a woodcut by Lionel Feininger : " Landscape." $4\frac{1}{8} \times 5\frac{1}{2}$ in. [146]

MacKnight Kauffer's often reproduced woodcut "Flight" [143], ultimately enlarged as a design and used as a hoarding poster, shows structural aims reduced to their geometrical basis. "Flight" represents the rapid winged movement of birds, and though uninteresting as a specimen of xylography, offers a useful diagrammatic illustration of modern tendencies. The eye, as it looks at this cut, is compelled to perform a journey along the lines and planes of the print; the movement thus executed by the eye alone for the purpose of enjoying "art" is not unlike the movement of the whole body on a waterchute, or—if curves were present in "Flight"—on a "switch-back"—performed for the purpose of enjoying "life." The analogy goes even further, for whilst art in which the "subject matter" is the main purpose may be compared with a railway journey undertaken for the purpose of reaching a destination, that modern art, which stresses design, may be compared with the rectilinear, or curvilinear movement of "chute" or switchback journey, which is undertaken merely for the sake of sensation and leads to no outside destination.

183

From a woodcut by Paul Vera : " Headpiece." 6 × 1½ in. [82]

Woodcuts of these Parisian types, with inflections towards the emotional or the intellectual, are produced by all cutters, of whatever nationality, who have come under the indirect influence of Cézanne and his posthumous " School." The interest in such work consists technically in the fact that they avoid xylographic *tours de force;* they are nearly all designs which, for pleasure or convenience, have been cut in wood or linoleum by the simplest possible methods. Amongst these *" le seul dont le dessin surgit impeccable sous la trame volontairement cubiste "* as a French writer claims, is Antoine-Pierre Gallien, " Peintre à la ligne noire " as he calls himself. Gallien is undoubtedly one of the most masterly designers in wood of the younger generation. *" Il ne sollicite pas : il impose "* as another French writer puts it ; but it is true. No matter what style he adopts, and Gallien can produce woodcuts that resemble orthodox and simple pen-line sketches (*e.g.*, Portrait of Rabindranath Tagore) or impressionistic designs in planes of black and white (*e.g.*, Portrait of the expressionist painter, Zadkine [144] ; he can, *incredibile dictu,* even translate Eugène Carrière into bold black and white lines and masses (*e.g.*, Portrait of Verlaine) with success. His " 20 Bois " are cubistic, and other abstract variations on a single theme : " nuditas " presenting its gamut from sensual to purely intellectual and unrepresentational abstraction. In the 26 " compositions " that accompany Paul Husson's " 18 proses-poèmes " he displays a variety of moods with extraordinary success and complete mastery [145]. Assuredly, however, he is greatest as a portraitist, whether he practises Holbeinesque sobriety (Rafael Lozano), impressionistic dash (Archipenko) or rank, but intentional absurdities (Portrait of Jean Tauzin, or the ridiculous head that decorates the catalogue of his Exhibition in the Boulevard Montparnasse).

An antithesis to him, an artist who manifestly produces with considerable difficulty and delights in technical *finesses*, is Galanis.

184

From J. E. Laboureur's woodcut illustration for a Series: "Images de l'arrière."
5½ × 5 in.   [146A]

From a woodcut by Galanis: "La Chasse." $4\frac{3}{4} \times 4\frac{1}{4}$ in. [148]

186

Galanis is a Greek painter, living in Paris, who has devoted much of his time to xylography, out of which medium he has got a quality peculiar to himself. His " vitalizing emotions " leave me as a rule entirely cold : what is interesting is purely and simply the form in which he embodies them. Galanis' landscapes, still-lifes and figures, though not distorted like Laboureur's [146A] or the Parisian Fleming Vlaminck's, or the German Feininger's cuts [146], are engraved on hard wood mainly for the pleasure of using tool and material. If one is not deeply moved by the artist's subject, one can, nevertheless, not withhold one's admiration for the way in which he invests these designs with xylographic qualities. Beginning with the professional trade xylographer's composite tint tool he worked at first rather amateurishly in a white line manner, so that one is never quite certain of the light and shade values which appear to be, though they are not, actually inverted, as in a negative. In an album, "Quatre Gravures," published in 1919, we, however, get interesting still-life compositions in which the artist, without in any way disguising his means, makes the eye enjoy not only its perambulations amongst white and black shapes in all their gradations of greyness, but also the " tactile " values of different textures. In a still more recent development he exchanges tone for line cutting, and his headpieces and tailpieces have a curious " Regency "-like bluffness, which many will find effective. Works illustrated by him include " Voyage musical au pays du passe," by Romain Rolland (Paris, Edouard Jeysot), " Deuil des Primères " (Paris, Crès) and readers of the French magazine " L'amour de l'art," from which these details are taken (Sept., 1921), will be familiar with his typographic ornaments [147], which are virtually still-life compositions of such objects as the eighteenth-century house and book decorator specially delighted in.

Galanis' woodcuts are decorative ; his admiration for cubistic intellectual abstraction having made way to more naturalistic representation, which gives, nevertheless, an impression of old-fashionedness [148].

One of the leaders of the decorative xylography [149] is, this time, a real Frenchman, Raoul Dufy,

From a woodcut by Raoul Dufy for the " Almanach des Lettres et des Arts." Original size.   [149]

187

From a woodcut by Morin-Jean : " Orphée."   6½ × 8 in.   [151]

whose light and fluid touch as a water-colour painter and designer for textiles, would hardly lead one to expect the virile qualities displayed in the set of cuts illustrating the pleasures of peace, hunting, fishing, dancing and—need one say it—" l'amour." The exhibition of this latter subject in England, I have reason to know, nearly led to a conflict with the " authorities," perhaps rightly. I will not express any judgment, except to point out that Dufy had certainly offended against the English formula in which such subjects may be presented to the English public without offence.   Dufy had given his composition an aesthetic *cachet* instead of a mincing or sentimental " *cachette*." The whole series was, at all events, informed with a sound sense of decorative values, both in line and mass, in arrangement and balance, a sense which gave the prints too an old-fashioned appearance. Other cuts of his are " La Comtesse de Ponthie "

188

From a woodcut by Raoul Dufy: "La Puce." One of the illustrations
for Guillaume Appolinaire's "Le Bestiaire." $4\frac{5}{8} \times 4\frac{3}{8}$ in. [150]

From a woodcut by Edgard Tijtgat : One of the illustrations
for "Little Red Riding Hood." 3¾ × 3½ in.   [152]

and " Le bestiaire ou le cortège d'Orphée " (Paris Editions de la
Sirène) with Guillaume Appolinaire's delightful rhymes. Dufy's
sense of humour and inexhaustible inventiveness as a maker of
patterns is in the latter amusingly displayed [150].
Another French xylographer who has a keen sense of decorative
composition is Morin-Jean. In his naturalistic manner the uniformity
of his line gives an effect of weakness instead of the manifestly aimed-
at feeling of strength. In his abstract still-life, reproduced in the Belgian
" Selection," he lacks Galanis' finesse ; but the pattern of such a cut
as his " Orphée " has, in its somewhat Persian manner, a strong and
pleasing appeal to the eye [151].
The three examples of Morin-Jean's just cited illustrate the somewhat
distracting influence to which the modern experimental artist is constantly subjected. Technical *quality* which intrigued (a hateful but
useful word) the older generation has, generally speaking, ceased
to have any meaning for him. The younger generation of artists are
pre-eminently intellectual designers, or metaphysical analysts, who
stand in relation to nature not so much as awed worshippers as
inquisitive experimenters with a scientific turn of mind. But it is

190

From a woodcut illustration for G. Appolinaire's "L'Enchanteur Pourrissant,"
by André Derain.   [154]

easier for the scientist to make nature yield him what he seeks than for the artist to exert a similar mastery. The scientist after all can rely on logic to help him, but ultimately, and in the last resort, the artist has to come back willy-nilly to feeling. Much of this *modern* work then should be regarded as a light-hearted struggle against heavy odds, or, if you like, as bold ventures into forbidden regions. The Guardian Angel of Eden must have been Napoleon Bonaparte's first incarnation, if indeed one may speak of an Angel as incarnate. He at all events personifies that law of the *Code Napoléon* which says : "*La recherche de la paternité*

From a linoleum cut by Max Weber. 2⅜ × 2 in. [155]

est interdite." Contraventions against this law are a sure source of trouble, especially when the research leads close to the gates of " The First Cause." The human mind, however, is lured to this hopeless research as a migratory bird to the lamps of a lighthouse. So the artist venturers have pursued *knowledge,* have dug down to the " primitive " minds of the savage and the child, or have sent up balloons of observation into the regions of the transcendental absolute. The efforts of children have been taken and discussed very seriously. Almost, we were led to believe, that such work as that of the Viennese children under Professor Cisek, or of the English children at the Weybridge Village Hall school were better " art " than Raphael's " School of Athens," or Titian's " Sacred and Profane Love." That children imitate their elders, that they have in them a subconscious legacy of " imitation," that, therefore, children from the moment that they are conscious of drawing and modelling, of painting and building at all are different from their elders is a fallacy : they are lower down the ladder. They often rush in and snatch the palm where their elders fear to tread, because they, like the valiant V.C.'s, know so little of the game. Hence children's work, however interesting psychologically, physiologically, or whatever other application of logic there may be, are never works of conscious art, and should not be admired or even encouraged *in that sense.* That, however, is not to say that the adult artist may not learn from them : learn, in the main, to remember what long and generally *false* teaching had caused him to forget, *viz.,* that one must feel *before* one can create.

192

From a linoleum cut by Max Weber.
4¼ × 2 in.   [156]

One cannot, however, advocate the conscious adoption of the infantile view point by an adult. Such an adoption seems to have taken place in the outlook of the Fleming, Edgard Tijtgat. I very much doubt, however, that this woodcutter is, objectively, conscious of his position at all; I rather think that he takes his art as seriously as a child does. He does not know that he is not a " grown up " artist; if he did, he would not take such endless trouble and pains with his work, going to the length of not only cutting and printing the pictures, but also the text of his books. Judging, I admit, by deduction only, I conclude that he is very serious about his art, not as a " stunt," nor as an experiment in aesthetics, but purely and simply as a means of expressing things he has very much at heart : the love of children (" Le petit chaperon rouge " [152], " Le lendemain de St. Nicholas "), the memory of a friend (" Quelques images de la vie d'un artiste : à mon ami Richard Wouters "). These things are examples of genuine expression which have just a little touch of

From a woodcut by Emil Nolde : " Portrait of a Young Man." 6¾ × 4¾ in. [157]

that quality called by Blake's publishers "genius." But it is his sense of colour [153] rather than his design, which is weak, and his drawing, which is weaker, that helps, in the jargon of the stage, to " get it over over the footlights."

194

From a woodcut by Christian Rohlfs : " The Prisoner."   6¾ × 5¼ in.   [158]

From a linoleum cut by Horace Brodzky.

[159A]

Tijtgat's art then is not a consciously self-analytic catharsis—such as—to me at all events—much of continental expressionistic art seems to be ; neither is it like the interesting cuts of the French artist, André Derain [154], a veteran revolutionary, artistically decorative. The latter's illustrations for " L'Enchanteur Pourrissant " have a genuine decorative value, inspired as they are by Gauguinesquely " savage " prototypes, a value one can enjoy like Raoul Dufy's even without enquiry into their meaning. I should maintain the same of some monochrome and colour prints of Max Weber, the American wood-cutter evidently inspired by Derain. Weber has a fine sense of colour values and sometimes of a deeper quality, a calm and strange dignity [155, 156]. An artist whose work seems to have little meaning, apart from the considerable decorative value of his design, is Franz Marc, a follower of Kandinsky, quoted as one of Germany's most representative

196

From a woodcut by Heinrich Campendonck. 7 ×6¼ in. [159]

artists. Hans Baldung Grien's " Horses " seem to have inspired Marc
in the direction of seeking inspiration in the animal rather than the
human relation. Marc, however, is " pre-war " and dead. The war
artists—I do not mean the illustrators of the preliminary catastrophe,
but those who most clearly demonstrate its disintegrating and more
catastrophic influence—are men who have sought wood and linoleum
in order to give expression in a cathartic sense to their feelings—I
mention, out of a host of others, Nolde [157], Pechstein, Schmidt
Rotluff, Christian Rohlfs [158], E. C. Kirchner, Josef Ebers and
Heinrich Campendonck. Their work appears to me in a rising scale
pathogical. Campendonck's retirement upon his innermost ego—as he
imagines—gives birth to strange fancies [159]. These men are interesting in respect of the manner in which they have made the black surface
of the wood block tell the " disturbances " created in their mind by
the world of to-day. Regarded as reflections of the times they live in,
or as psychic adventures, these German prints are significant ; as
works of art they seem rather more convincing than kindred productions of other countries, such as Belgium for example, who have a
somewhat similar excuse. Cuts represented in " Selection," a Belgian
" Chronique de la Vie Artistique," by Jozef Cantré, Jean Colette,

197

From a linoleum cut by William Zorach: " Province Town." $10\frac{3}{4} \times 8\frac{3}{4}$ in.   [160]

198

From a linoleum cut by William Zorach : " Figures in a Landscape." $5\frac{1}{2} \times 9\frac{3}{4}$ in. [162]

Fritz van den Berghe, Louis Decoeur and several others, seem only pardonable if regarded as means of relief to the artist.

I have the same feeling in regard to the less abnormal American work, such as Louis Bouché's, or the slightly more decorative B. Gussow's, of New York. The mere cutting of white out of black, even the arranging of a more or less pleasing pattern is not in itself to the spectator a sufficient reason for the existence of such works of art—whatever it may be to the artist. The Australian, Horace Brodzky [159A], Gaudier Brzecka's friend, seems to have saner intentions. However, I am not able to follow expressionism in all its facets; but I admit that my eyes may be blind, my mind closed to its significance, and admit it the more willingly as the following story, which I have no reason to doubt, confirms the possibility of a " method in their madness." Professor Landsberger, in his " Impressionismus and Expressionismus,'" tells how Karin Michaelis, the novelist, called on Oscar Kokoschka, the leading German exponent of expressionism, and himself an able writer. Karin Michaelis saw in his studio the portrait of a young girl with a face that looked as if it were speckled with spots of coal dust. (One can imagine the sort of thing it must have been.) This curious " rash " the artist accounted for by telling his

¹Leipzig, 1919, Klinkhardt & Biermann.

199

From a linoleum cut by Marguerite Zorach : " Province Town Players." 7¾ × 11½ in. [163]

questioner that the model was so absent-minded that her face appeared to him like that. This extraordinary vision was, subsequently, explained or confirmed by the fact that the girl lost her reason, though no one suspected such a possibility at the time.

I only repeat the story because it may help to explain the weird " complexion " of this kind of continental " expressionism " of which we find fainter reflections in the " States." In the " States," however, we have also interesting examples of xylography which show a perfectly healthy desire of the artist to create a kind of personal " kosmos," a closely knit order created out of natural elements, but in accordance with the artist's own consciousness. There is, it is true, something in the nature of a " title " which establishes a literary association, but the *subject* is, nevertheless, only to be comprehended as a design. The artists who most appeal to me in this respect are William Zorach and his wife Marguerite. William Zorach's compositions are broad white on black designs, in which representational simplification is counterbalanced by a decorative interplay of black and white shapes.

200

From a linoleum cut by William Zorach: "The Pool." $10\frac{3}{4} \times 14$ in.

[161]

From a linoleum cut by Walt. Kuhn : "Fecundity." 6¼ ×8 in.
[164]

His "Pool" [161], his "Province Town" [160], his "Sailing," and above all his "Figures in a Landscape" [162], are all courageous adventures in creative design. Marguerite Zorach's "Province Town Players"[163], though not quite as well composed as her husband's work, is not seen at its best in the reproduction, which has lost its half-tone along the contours. Somewhat similar aims are pursued by Walt Kuhn in his "Fecundity" [164], whilst the same artist's "Odalisques" [165] is full of movement, but either too realistic or not realistic enough to be convincing. Another American, C. Bertram Hartmann for instance, succeeds in his carefully considered, but somewhat geometrically designed, cuts precisely because his more abstract forms do not challenge unnecessary comparisons with "nature." His "Girl on Horseback" [166] is a swinging arrangement of flat pattern reminiscent of Greek vase painting strangely conjoined with modern cubism, which is even more pronounced in the, to me less satisfactory, cut of "Man and Horse."

As to the often incredibly coarse

From a linoleum cut by C. Bertram Hartmann :
"Girl on Horseback." 9½×7 in.   [166]

202

From a linoleum cut by Walt. Kuhn : "Odalisques."   8 ×7½ in.   [165]

and primitive or childlike, whatever their significance otherwise,
there is, however, at least this to be said : they state facts without
circumlocution—in the fewest possible lines—there is not one line
that could be left out without making the omission immediately
obvious. If we compare, for example, such a specimen of wood
engraving as done in the famous "sixties" as M. A. Williams'
representation of "Sidney's Tree" [167], not with one of the expressionistic line cuts of the Continent, but with such a very *mild*

203

From a wood engraving by M. A. Williams of J. T. Horn's design: "Sidney's Tree." 1860. Original size.   [167]

form of modern simplification as Philip Hagreen's "Wind" [168], we notice at once that in Hagreen's cut each mark of the tool has more significance than a dozen in Williams' minute rendering of nature: Williams supplies an inventory in sentimental prose; Hagreen gives us, as it were, a few lines of sensible poetry.

If, on the other hand, it is imagined that the Victorian engravers did not know their job, technically, and that by the mere fact of designing white on black with the tool itself the woodcut becomes "truly original," that is a grave mistake. The set of woodcuts recently done by Lionel Lindsay apparently in this belief are, especially considering the circumstances in which they came about in far away Australia, commendable enough, but their technique cannot be compared for quality with the work done by the professional wood engravers of the Victorian age.

204

From a woodcut by Philip Hagreen: "The Wind."
1921. Slightly reduced. [168]

By pushing Hagreen's technique of simplification still further, and by lowering the quality of experience to the level of Matisse's " Five Year Old," [1] or by even letting it go entirely into the subconscious, one gets the kind of " expressionism " just referred to in German or Belgian examples.

On the other hand, by raising the quality of experience from conscious optic impression to conscious mental expression, and by pushing the technique up the scale until it responds to the quality of *mental* experience (not the objective optic experience of the impressionists), we get the kind of landscape the brothers Paul and John Nash express in wood. Paul Nash has quite recently published a little book of seven woodcuts called " 7 Places," which are the best of this kind of ego-centric art so far done in England. Each of the seven places is accompanied by a little prose-poem written by the artist and intended to illustrate the print. I am not sure that they are very successful, either as literary or illustrative efforts ; it is in any case extremely doubtful whether words can *explain* pictures, whilst pictures that explain words thereby cease to belong to the category of creative expression. Apart from the text the cuts are beautiful examples of imaginative design. Such a print as

[1] The impressionists aimed at the optic level of a cow ; Matisse, at the mental vision of a five-year-old child—that is, at all events, an " advance."

205

From a woodcut by Paul Nash : " Dyke by the Road." 4¾×7 in. [170]

" Black Poplars " [169], for instance, has both chromatic and plastic,
i.e., two and three dimensional invention. In a still later cut, and in
some respects better cut, " Dyke by the Road " [170], Paul Nash is
experimenting with a rather different glyptic manner and a composition that is stronger in spatial recession. All this kind of art is in
the nature of experiment, of aesthetic adventure, and this one feels by
the manner in which it deals with the human figure. Here its tentative-
ness is manifest. For whilst it pretends to distinguish between aesthetic
and associative emotion, or between aesthetic sensibility and literary
sentimentality, the very theme of such a cut as Nash's " Way into the
Wood," and the very treatment of his figures generally indicate not
only the close connection between the two forms of *sensing*, but also
the artist's manifest difficulty in finding a satisfactory formula for
the "transfiguration" of the human figure, corresponding to his
transfiguration of nature.
John Nash has perhaps not the same intellectual force and independence
of spirit as his brother Paul, but there is more sensitiveness and a more

206

From a woodcut by Paul Nash : " Black Poplars."   6 × 4½ in.   [169]

207

From a woodcut by John Nash : "Sheep Shearing." 4¾×6 in.   [172]

vital glyptic quality in his cutting [173]. A comparison between Paul's
" Winter Wood " and John's " Wood Interior " [171] will explain
both the similarities and the differences between their work better than
words. John gets more cubic weight with his design and into the actual
quality of his excisions. Comparison between Brangwyn's [94] and
John Nash's [172] " Sheep Shearing " cuts and Norman Janes' " Sheep
Barn in Surrey " [174] will divulge different shades of glyptic vitality.
Amongst the artists of the younger generation in England who have
turned more resolutely to simpler ideals and whose *style*, moreover,
is hailed as distinctly English is Ethelbert White. English enough
his style is if we mean by that a certain frank simplicity and stiffness
and precision ; yet it could never have come about but for the reaction
which set in during the first decade of this century against pictorial

208

From a woodcut by Norman Janes: "Sheep Barn in Surrey." 8¾ × 6¼ in. [174]

impressionism and literary aestheticism. Interesting as White's earlier cuts may be as regards simplification and designed cutting, he is beginning to show his real metal not so much in the pleasant earlier illustrations of Fish Stalls, of Punch and Judy Shows, English Horsemen [175] and English Landscapes, but in his last cut " The Old Barn " [176]. This is a little masterpiece of engraving: it is designed in wood : it is engraved without worrying the material, every cut is clean, sound and carefully premeditated. It is less " solid," but more naturalistic than Paul Nash's work—it is simpler ; it has a greater glyptic quality and an individual atmosphere of brilliant light.

In all these " expressionistic " woodcuts the usual objects, though distorted, or simplified, grouped, divided and reassembled in a new aesthetic order, are still recognizable. In strictly cubistic art, to which they owe their existence, the objects themselves are dissected, but so far as I am aware, there are no truly cubistic and, therefore, abstract designs in xylography, and as may be found in drawing, painting and

HH

209

sculpture. If such highly intellectual and objective performances have not been designed in wood, though some of Gallien's come near it, abstraction on a strictly emotional and subjective basis has been practised by an artist and writer whose theories are part of the substructure of modern experimental art. This artist, Wassili Kandinsky, a Russian Pole who has lived in Germany most of his life, has written a great deal about his outlook. He is the defender of intuition; of the subconscious. He believes that there are " spiritual harmonies " to which the artist by eliminating intellectual control can give utterance. He believes in a pictorial art as unrepresentational as music, and he has sublimated his faith in paintings and woodcuts, which are as little "naturalistic" and representational as Picasso's cubistic syntheses of form, but from the very opposite causes. Picasso's cubism is entirely logical; Kandinsky's is purely emotional [177, 177A], albeit decked with a panoply of literary and semi-scientific explanation. His colour sense, both in theory and practice, is keen; his sense of form apparently lacking. In his black and white woodcuts, however, he uses the two opposites with considerable decorative effect. What exactly the forms represent or symbolize is quite uncertain [178]; nevertheless, the designs have the quality of visions as one experiences in the half-consciousness of dreams and vainly seeks to recall on awakening. Kandinsky's woodcuts, and for that matter his painted " compositions," mark the attempt of man to reach his inner life and to turn it inside out, just as cubism marks the attempt to see his environment, to comprehend it, by turning it concentrically outside in, the centre being the individual. In so far as actual objects of vision are deprived in both processes of recognizable representation and their *disjecta membra* fail to unite once more in the spectator's mind, both attempts constitute of necessity a failure. But these " polar expeditions " by which man has tried to explore the nature of his own polarity, though failures in themselves, have yet had positive results. The greatest of these so far as art is concerned is the conviction that the artist is not *vis-à-vis* but part and parcel of " nature," and that therefore it can neither be his task to *imitate* her, in Leonardo's, nor to " *correct* her defects and blemishes " in Reynolds' sense. He *uses* her. If there be any question of imitation and correction it is ultimately one of " re-producing " and correcting his own self.

210

From a woodcut by John Nash: " Wood Interior." $4\frac{3}{4} \times 8$ in.

From a Russian woodcut published in " The Black Year " (1922) : " Cottages without the Thatches, which have been eaten by Peasants." 2 ×6 in. [204]

THE ELEVENTH CHAPTER: THE RETURN TO LITERARY AND ASSOCIATIVE CONTENT

THE new orientation of humanity averted from the past is towards the future; and the new freedom of art means its emancipation from the tyranny of tradition. The Rome of Michael Angelo has ceased with the Venice of Titian, or the Athens of Phidias, to hold the last word in art. Egypt and Crete have opened their lips ; China, Japan and Mexico, Bushman and Stoneman have spoken, infants have stammered, and we have understood the significance of their *forms*, if not all the meaning of their *contents*. That indeed has been our failing : an inordinate interest in *form* with a progressive weakening of content: an intellectual exercise of the mind. Kandinsky tried to get at the *content* without intellectual surveillance : and those who have followed him have created works which are not far removed from the work of minds that have irretrievably lost the power of surveillance—lunatics. So the present generation turns its attention once more to the expression of *contents* of greater import than haystacks in a mist, or apples on a crumpled napkin.

Perhaps the best example, and in any case the only one known to me, in which artistic form is made to cover literary expression is the work of the Fleming, Frans Masereel.

Even a casual glance at his woodcuts will show that his design has been strongly influenced by French cubistic theories. Nevertheless, he is a true son of the country that produced a Peter Brugehel and a Jerome Bosch. He uses the medium in order to illustrate contemporary ideas, his own life, his own thought, his own environment.

212

From a woodcut by Ethelbert White : " The Sportsman."   5½×7 in.   [175]

Moreover, he does this in the very Flemishly frank manner of the earlier artists. He says exactly what he thinks and with remarkable aptness finds convincing images for every thought. These images are enshrined in small *cuts* devoid of half-tones, done rapidly and following one another along a continuous thread. No text accompanies his story, which is told in multiple composition [1] with subtlety and humour, and wit that is at times bitter and tragic. To Masereel, indeed, the woodcut is what the manuscript page is to the writer, and, in consequence of the technique he uses, it probably does not take him much more time to *cut* a novel in wood than it would take a writer to put it into words : only that the artist can express what the

[1] By "multiple composition" I mean an ideological composition which dispenses with natural perspective and unites in one and the same design images of passing thoughts in the order of their mental rather than optical importance—after the manner of Dürer and the earlier artists. Only that, thanks to modern aesthetic experiments, the composition as such preserves an immediately optic unity.

213

writer cannot express, so that the analogy is not perfect of course. In "Le Soleil," [179] a book of sixty-seven cuts, dedicated to his wife, we are made to follow a dream of the artist signifying in the truly Freudian manner an analysis of unfulfilled desires. We see the artist asleep at his desk ; his spirit takes flight, quite in the manner of primitive Christian art as a diminutive replica of its owner, out of the window. The street crowd, however, mistakes the spirit for the body which falls into the street. He rises, takes to his heels through the town, out of it, pointing to the sun. Seeking refuge from his pursuers he darts

From a woodcut by John Nash.
2¾ × 2 in.   [173]

into a house, upstairs, on to the roof, up the chimney . . . . . thus we become interested in the adventures of a spirit seeking the light, and the adventures, that is to say his desires, take him to the Church, where he mistakes the nimbus for the sun, drag him down through drinking dens and brothels to prison and to fairs, to tree tops and corn fields, to the ocean, to ship and masthead, whence he falls into the depths of the sea, encounters an octopus, a mermaid, climbs a lighthouse, soars sunwards and bursts into flames . . . . . thus he falls on to his own desk, surprises himself as he realizes that he has awakened from a dream—the dream of the spirit seeking freedom.

This bare and fragmentary outline is only intended to tell of the manner in which it is done a little more fully than may be deducible from a few detached illustrations.

This is only one book of sixty-seven cuts. " Mon livre d'heures " contains, however, one hundred and sixty-seven. Another such " novel " is his " Histoire sans paroles." In addition to such books he has illustrated numerous others. Fifty-seven cuts illustrate Verhaeren's poems, twenty-five " L'Hotel-dieu," by P. J. Jouve, thirty-two Romain Rolland's " Liberté," twenty-seven " Le Bien Commun," by R. Arcos, who is the publisher of the " Editions du Sablier," in which all these things have appeared.

Let me in conclusion quote M. P. J. Jouve : [1]

> " Une ' Passion ' dans le cadre contemporain, une suite sur l'Eternel Feminin, et des fantaisies des ' diableries ' et

[1] In Dix Gravures sur Bois du " Nouvel Essor," Paris.

214

From a woodcut by Ethelbert White : " The Old Barn."   5½ × 8¼ in.

From a woodcut by Wassili Kandinsky, from " Klänge." [177A]

hallucinations modernes, scènes de la revolution ou de la Bourse, du journal ou de la pègre, qui étonnent, suffoquent presque et parfois inquiètent par leur intensité ; Masereel ne s'arrête pas là ; il a de plus grands rêves. Ce constructeur de livres pourrait aussi devenir un jour constructeur de Fresques . . . . . "
The distance we have travelled since Ricketts in the " Nineties " revived the " Original Wood Engraving " for book illustration, could not be better shown than by comparison of the English artist's delicate aestheticism and the Fleming's robust topicality ; Ricketts' calligraphy, detached and painstaking, Masereel's shorthand, passionate and abrupt. Where here is the relevance of aesthetic standards ? Or, should we not perhaps say : are aesthetic standards ever real, ever even possible : is it not always at bottom Life we must measure ; and that being so,

216

Reproduction of four pages of the picture-story "Le Soleil" by Frans Masereel.   [179]

II   **217**

From a woodcut by Emilio Mantelli : " Fonti Ignorante." 4 × 5⅝ in.

who could doubt that there is more LIFE in Masereel ? " Il a pour lui," continues M. Jouve, " son extraordinaire volonté modeste qui est celle d'un artisan de cathédrales."

"Artisan de Cathédrales "—here we are reminded of that instinctive feeling which naturally exalts the modest artisan working anonymously in the service of a spiritual idea above the artist solving consciously and name-proud an egocentric problem of aesthetics.

Masereel may stand as a symbol of the old wine entering new bottles: for he is one of those to whom art is not an empty vessel to be admired for its shape: rather would he prize it for its contents.

And this is true of an increasing number of modern artists. This reaching out for " the Sun " and the clothing of " the Passion " in a modern garb comes now with greater force, with greater insistance and also with greater contempt for surface beauty. " To look upon things for the sake of their external beauty is to be corrupt in spirit " says one of these artists with Biblical bitterness.

218

Horace Gerrard—" Marriage of Rebecca."

[181]

From a woodcut by Marcia Lane Foster for Anatole
France's " Merrie Tales of Jacques Tournebroche."
Original size.   [183]

Dogmatic Churches and more or less established Creeds, as kinds of
transcendental cradles and spiritual crèches, are looming once more
large in the consciousness of humanity because it is—for the moment
—baffled by its own apparent impotence. Man has lost faith in himself,
and in the True God within : so he turns either cynically from " all
the creeds

and counts himself no more than a blown leaf "
as the poet, F. S. Flint does in a fine frenzy of scepsis ; or, on the
contrary, seeks balm and protection in some external, established
form of " Faith."

It is, then, hardly surprising that a number of woodcutters have had
recourse to the Bible, which gives back what we bring to it in a
form made beautiful by its language and association, and topical
by its accounts of the everlasting conflict between the individual and
the herd.

The troubled conscience of thinking humanity has found its reflection
also in the humble craft of woodcutting. What, however, makes this
reflection interesting is the great variety in which, owing to the aesthetic
currents and cross-currents of our times the subject finds expression, and
the varying depth of feeling and earnestness which it makes manifest.

220

From a woodcut by Marcia Lane Foster for Anatole
France's " Merrie Tales of Jacques Tournebroche."
Original size.   [184]

We find, for example, in Brangwyn's " Via Dolorosa " [92], an indict-
ment of common humanity rather unjustly, I think, symbolized by a
purely " working class " environment. This woodcut is, nevertheless,
the best of all this artist's cuts. Brangwyn's strength as an artist lies
in the fact that he works on the spur of emotions and applies his
intellect to the practical problems these set him.
The reverse is the case in Eric Gill's work. Gill is a craftsman with
intellectual theories of life and art, a mind that has embraced catholicism
with his intellect where in Brangwyn it is an inborn emotional complex.
We find, therefore, in Gill's design, an ineradicable self-consciousness,
a sense of personal value and importance which were objectionable
but for the fact that the artist never spares himself ; the slightest thing
he does is executed with meticulous care and with an intellectual nicety
that divides his art by a world's width from Brangwyn's. Whatever
emotions he may possess they have passed as it were through a narrow

221

From a woodcut by Christopher Perkins : "Apollo and Diana." A design for a plate. 8½ × 8½ in. [185]

purging flame of intellectual white-heat before they reach the material in which he happens to be working. I say narrow flame, because his intellectual capacity seems keen rather than broad. As a xylographer he shows no sign of sympathy with the material ; his engraving is done with perfect precision and control on hard wood with a sharp tool and might with equal aesthetic result be done in metal ; indeed some of his prints, such as the " Christ driving out the money changers," look almost like a rubbing from a Church brass. The style of his design outwardly associated, now with Byzantine rigour, anon with sensuous freedom and cut in the simplest and nakedest of white lines with extraordinary skill and Euclidian precision, is aesthetically unimpeachable. Gill's conception of the function of his art is that it should furnish the intellectual substructure for the emotional or religious requirements of the spectator.

Hence his " Stations of the Cross," "Crucifixions," "Nativities," are ingenious variations of their different themes, beautifully composed, firmly designed and carefully printed, but intellectual abstractions, black and Byzantine on a white surface : his lights are dark, his darks the light of nature. He produces, as it were, the negative which, in his intention, shall imprint itself positively upon the mind of the spectator, whom, however, he leaves the task of filling in the details of expression and modelling—*ad libitum*.

222

From a woodcut by Christopher Perkins : From a series
of illustrations for the New Testament. 6 ×6½ in. [186]

Gill's relation to his craft, or rather to his public—made more complicated by occasional excursions into what one may perhaps describe
as a mystic kind of sensuality—is one of sentimental intellectualism.
" It is, of course, impossible to stem the tide of commercial degradation
until Poverty, Chastity and Obedience take the place of Riches,
Pleasure and ' Laissez faire '," he says in the introduction to a pamphlet
on wood engraving by R. J. Beedham. It is the obverse of the darkest
ages : the reverse of which was " of course " " Riches, Pleasure and
'Laissez faire'" in the hands and minds of those to whom the poor,
the chaste and the obedient were slavishly and superstitiously subject.[1]
The case of other English artists of the younger generation, such as
Stanley Spencer, F. M. Medworth and Ethelbert White, all of whom
have engraved religious subjects in wood, is not so clear. Their cuts
—and their paintings for that matter—are exercises in design more
certainly than expressions of religious feeling. Rather more convincing in this respect are some religious and symbolical subjects
engraved by Horace Gerrard. Gerrard is a highly skilled technician,

[1]Unfortunately, I am unable to illustrate Gill's work, because he objects to what he calls the " pseudo-
    facsimile " of the photographic *line* block, whilst my aesthetic conscience will not allow me to mar
    the significance of his work by the half-tone process, which tends to reduce both black and white
    to grey, a deterioration to which, nevertheless, the artist would not appear to object.

223

From a woodcut by F. M. Medworth: Study in
white line. 3 ×4 in.   [187B]

whose zoological and medical wood engravings vie in competence with
the work of the old professional reproductive engraver. His
translations of Central American sculpture into the xylographic form of a
black and white pattern are in an aesthetic sense even more interesting
as demanding a creative technique [180]. The Biblical subject, here
reproduced representing "The Marriage of Rebecca "[181], is proof
of an original view point. The combination of the white contours of
the figures in the foreground and the treatment of the foliage and
landscape, with the massed white line of the principal group and the
bold gouging of the sky are distinctly personal elements of design.
Gerrard's work is full of great promise not yet quite fulfilled, because
he has set himself a most difficult problem—the exploitation of the
white contour line as light-colour *and* pattern bearer.

We have seen the difficulty of the white contour design in Urs Graf's
sixteenth-century cuts. A number of modern artists have set themselves
similar problems. Amongst these Gordon Craig's recent theatrical
figures, cut in bold white lines on soft wood, deserve first mention.
Craig is an artist to his fingertips. These white line cuts, " Ophelia,"
" Hamlet and Daemon," " Old Gobbo," and others, though their
white is often a shadow and their black a light, are " geistreich " in
conception and executed not only with great skill but with that nice
economy of effort which distinguishes the master from the labourer
and the 'prentice.

They are, however, not " contour line cuts " in the strict sense.

How difficult the proper use of the white *contour* really is may be

224

From a woodcut series by Alice
D. Laughlin: "Pierrot at the
Grave of Columbine." 1¾ × 1¾ in.
[188]

pupil of J. J. Murphy, whose interesting work we shall presently have
to discuss. Miss Laughlin uses, in the little " Pierrot "[188] series, of
which an example is here reproduced, her graver with great skill and
an almost stenographic economy of line to express a maximum of
emotion with a minimum of means. Such things are, however, little
tours de force that are curiosities rather than works of art. Her more
elaborate, less sentimental and Murphy-inspired cuts prove, indeed,
that she has less to say than these miniatures might lead one to expect.
More disciplined and indeed expressive is Cecile Buller's (Mrs. J. J.
Murphy) work, which we may here note because it too is influenced
strongly by the same master. Her " Jugglers " [189] is quite remarkable for the sense of motion in the rhythm of the bouncing balls.
Returning once more to the white contour line : a compatriot of theirs,
Henry Fitch Taylor, has made extremely simple, but decorative and
effective use of this line in a number of linoleum cuts [190]. They are
printed in orange and brown tints so that the weight of colour does
not kill the white lines, which are "few and far between," but, nevertheless, so firmly and organically connected that they constitute fine
aesthetic compositions of a pronounced sculpturesque quality ; Taylor
is, as one would suspect, a sculptor of acknowledged merit and these
prints of his have, in spite of incongruous Gauguinesque Tahiti-ism,
considerable aesthetic value. The mention of Gauguin links another
American, George Biddle, to this group ; his Tahitian cuts [190A] are
bold black and white patterns which show Gauguin's influence not
only in choice of subject, but also in a certain " savage " style.
Amongst English artists, Rupert Lee, when he does not allow his
whimsicality to have the better of him, as in " wooden " tigers and

227

From a woodcut by Cecile Buller: "The Jugglers." 4½ × 5 in.   [189]

the weird "Rider on a Bull" [191B], which is derived from the accidental shape of a bit of scrap-iron, rises in his "Spider Monkeys," [191] to considerable aesthetic achievement. Robert Young, a protagonist of the modern movement in America, has found in the form of a nigger's black body [192] inspiration for a white on black design which has fundamentally no more "content" than Lee's "Spider Monkeys," from which it differs mainly in a less brilliant invention of composition, and in the nature of the cutting, which in Lee's case was done on hard wood with a graver. That nigger bodies —not, be it observed, "Uncle Tom"-like souls—that monkeys and scrap-iron, could *inspire* the artists of to-day is a further proof of the distance which separates us from the art of the day before yesterday. Nevertheless, even the most experimental and coldly intellectual of them are dissatisfied.

For the younger generation, however, the transition from *form* as the "vitalizing emotion," to *content, i.e.,* from the shape of the bottle

228

From a linoleum cut by Henry Fitch Taylor : " Man on Horseback." 12 ×9 in.

From a woodcut by Rupert Lee: "The Rider."
$7\frac{3}{4} \times 6\frac{3}{4}$ in. [1918]

to the bouquet of the wine is, after decades of abstinence, a new and irksome problem. Some, like the American, Rockwell Kent, have, after experimenting in other directions, taken the step by boldly adopting both subject and treatment from an admired prototype—in this case, Blake [193]. A far more independent attempt to stress content, and to pour the old spirit of the Gospel into a new " bottle " has been recently made by the American wood engraver, J. J. A. Murphy. This is somewhat surprising, so far as this particular artist is concerned, seeing that his experiments in xylography are otherwise manifestly prompted by form rather than content [194]. J. J. Murphy was for some time an assistant to Frank Brangwyn ; but returning to the States he became one of the pioneers of the woodcut as a substitute for the process block in advertising. His poster for the American Navy and some commercial advertisements particularly show a Brangwynesque virility and also formulae of composition favoured by the English artist. After trying picturesque naturalistic design, Murphy adopted a linear convention which was at first not much more than the professional engraver's " tint " line technique many times enlarged. In his present phase Murphy—still favouring parallel white lines for the purpose of expressing plastic and chromatic values, tends

230

From Robert Young's linoleum cut: "The Bather." $8\frac{3}{8} \times 6\frac{1}{2}$ in.   [192]

From a linoleum cut by George Biddle : " Tahiti."   4½ × 7 in.   [190A]

to curtail them and apply them in square formations. It is true that by
such means he gets more light and colour, and altogether three-
dimensional values into his prints than any other xylographer known to
me ; but his formula is too insistent. His earlier naturalistic work, such
as for example a cut reproduced in the American magazine "The Play
Boy," and representing a soldier going " over the top," was in many
respects inferior to his new manner, but it attacked problems which
the new technique seems to me to evade rather than to solve.

As a Catholic, it is Murphy's ambition to produce one hundred
different versions of the Nativity, of which he has so far completed
eleven and of which the second is the best. When we get this artist on
a religious subject we know, even if we had no other means of doing
so, that he is sincere : utmost sincerity and frankness is implicit in
his technique. We also know, from his other work, that he will—after
the manner of Eric Gill—treat his religious subjects on an intellectual
plane, aiming consciously at simplicity of means. In contrast to Gill,
however, the American has a great sense of colour, and the " Nativity "
just mentioned, and a great many others, are remarkable for this
particular quality of its black and white. Much time, thought, skill
and painstaking care have been brought to bear on the execution of the

231

From a woodcut by Rockwell Kent. 6×6 in.   [193]

little white line engravings representing the fourteen Stations of the
Cross [195] which, to do them justice, should be seen in their
entirety. The tragedy unfolds itself, in spite of the gnat-like proportions, with perfect clearness, the figures move and are moved by
the emotions they visualize, and the landscape changes its mood in
sympathy with these. Anyone who follows this " Passion " from
station to station with diligence, will understand it intellectually,
and will appreciate it aesthetically as much as his remarkable cut
232

From a woodcut by Rupert Lee: "Spider Monkeys." Slightly reduced.   [191]

A woodcut by J. J. A. Murphy : From a series : " The Way
of the Cross."   3 × 3½ in.   [195]

234

From a woodcut by J. J. A. Murphy: "Father, Mother, Son." 5¼×4¾ in. [194]

From a woodcut by J. J. A. Murphy : "Shadowed Faces."   3 × 4½ in.   [196]

236

From a woodcut by Gustav Wolf : "The Third Day of Creation," one of a series illustrating "The Book of Genesis." 7½ × 5½ in.   [197]

237

From a woodcut by Josef Weiss: "Dives and Lazarus." $8\frac{1}{2} \times 7\frac{1}{4}$ in.   [200]

238

From a woodcut by Bruno Goldschmidt: " After the Fall," one of the series of Bible illustrations.
$16\frac{1}{2} \times 11\frac{3}{4}$ in.

[202]

From a woodcut by Bruno Goldschmidt : "Moses Changing Water into Blood," one of a series of Bible illustrations.   11¾ × 16½ in.   [203]

called "Shadowed Faces" [196], perhaps not quite as much in fact, because "Shadowed Faces" is in respect of colour, form, and particularly its three dimensional composition, as well as in the technical means by which these are created, an aesthetically better thing. This praise, however, contains by implication also a criticism: it means that the artist has intellectually more to say than emotionally. He feels, in common with many "modern" artists, his art as a problem rather than as a medium, *i.e.*, a means to an end outside "art," or to use a simile already employed, a switchback ride rather than a train journey.

And this is not surprising. America has not suffered like Europe, and in Europe again it is the countries which have lost the war and suffered most materially and spiritually who are experiencing most emotion in the choice and treatment of their subjects.

It is the Austrian and German artists who lose themselves in vague cosmic dreams and apocalyptic ecstasies.

240

From E. Schlangenhausen's linoleum cut: " Peace, be Still ! "   Reduced.

From E. Schlangenhausen's linoleum cut: "Die Rehe." Reduced. [199]

Perhaps the most serious of these is Gustav Wolf, to whom the woodcut, as indeed every form of drawing, is not representation or imitation of " nature " nor decoration in the ordinary sense—but the making of signs and symbols of what he regards as the ultimate realities. The page illustrating the third day of Creation from his " Illustration for the Book of Genesis " [197] will give an indication of his qualities.

Another artist who moves in a similar world of transcendental ideas is an Austrian woman, E. Schlangenhausen. The titles of her sets of woodcuts are a sufficient indication of her aims. There are, amongst others, " The Words of Christ " [198], " The Days of Creation," " The Longing for the Sun," " The Ways of the Stars," " The Eye of God." Such subjects spring from other than purely aesthetic emotions, though the artist shows that her forms of expression are connected with the school of Continental, i.e., ultimately Parisian theories of art. Her " Wild Horses " and " The Deer " [199] link her more immediately with Franz Marc's animal worship, but she gives to such themes a strongly sentimental cast. Her manner of printing with an excess of oil in her ink and thus producing an over-tone is a device much favoured abroad. Far from sentimental, but sombre and even, at times, gruesome, are the peculiar black line cuts of the German wood-sculptor, Ernst Barlach, whose heavy, though expressive, sculpture would hardly lead one to expect the effective, but really calligraphic, convention which he uses in xylography.

When, however, we come to technical means employed for the expression in woodcut of passionate feeling, the extraordinary work of Josef Weiss, of Munich, is far and away the most remarkable. He, too, has cut a series of Bible illustrations, amongst them the "Apocalypse" and "Genesis." Our illustrations [200, 201] will explain the quality of his imagination and technique better than words—both deserve careful study. Weiss is not yet thirty, is entirely self-taught and deliberately closes his eyes against any influences, whether from the old or the modern Masters. His talent is so pronounced that his achievement may conceivably remain unhurt by a form of prejudice which smacks a little of fear. A little more knowledge of orthodox draughtsmanship would, it seems to me, not hurt him. On the other hand, his obvious sincerity and the white-heat of his emotions raises his work, despite its faults [200], to higher levels. In the " Four Trumpets " [201] his way of handling the wood, lowering and scraping the surface as he does, almost in the manner of mezzotint, is entirely personal and admirable, whilst his conceptions have often

From a Russian woodcut published in " The Black Year " (1922) : " Hungry Wolves and Dead Men." 2 ×6 in.   [205]

a sensational grandeur which reminds one of El Greco and Blake. The Bible has inspired another " Central European," Bruno Gold-schmidt, to attempt a series of illustrations. He, too, is filled with cosmic visions and with phantasies of strange bitterness and emaciation, as his "After the Fall" [202] and " Moses changing water into blood," [203] here illustrated, may prove. "And there was blood throughout all the land of Egypt." The reason for the choice of just these subjects is not perhaps far to seek. The terror and bitterness becomes still greater when we contemplate such a humble piece of work as the one here [206] presented, a woodcut that has ceased to serve any aesthetic purpose and has become once more, as in the early days, a message which those who run may read. It was recently done in Russia and represents that glorious culmination of our present stage of civilization : a " man-eating " Russian. This cut and others here [204, 205] reproduced are taken from "Tchernaia Goduna"—the Black Year—a periodical dealing with all the aspects of the terrible famine. To those whom art is mainly an occupation for minds mentally at a loose end, these things should be particularly displeasing. These Russian Famine woodcuts have nothing to do with art, in so far as this word stands for conscious aesthetics. They are strictly utilitarian : their appeal is to our ethic or moral, rather than to our aesthetic sense : they are essentially sentimental. What, nevertheless, raises them to a higher level than the sentimental pictures, with which the world since the days of Greuze has been made familiar, is the absence of aesthetic trappings. It is the economy of means caused by a strict attention to and concentration upon the subject matter, the *content* of the cut which makes their *form* valuable.
It is claimed that these Russian cuts, as indeed the " Upheavalist " art of present-day Russia, in general, are made by members of the

242

From Josef Weiss' woodcut : " The Four Trumpets." Reduced.

Proletariat. The "Proletkult," of Moscow, have published an album, " Graphica," containing twenty woodcuts, all said to have been done by working men. In so far as these cuts represent an aesthetic effort, they are on an average no better than a similar effort would make them in countries which do not make a *cult* of the proletariat. Art has, as such, no part in class distinctions. Modern Russian xylography, in so far as I can judge, shows the same divisions that are manifest in all other : the good, the bad and the indifferent. The aspect of some of the best of these cuts suggests that, far from being the spontaneous result of primitive effort, they are the result of a conscious and effective economy in the means of expression, which is the outcome of modern aesthetic experiments, and these have their origins in Western Europe.

From a Russian woodcut published in "The Black Year" (1922): "Driven Mad by Starvation." Original size. [206]

From Horace Gerrard's xylographic translation of a piece of " Maya " sculpture.   [180]

CONCLUSION

 HAVE, in the foregoing, attempted to trace the various developments of one of the oldest, and, in a sense, simplest forms of multiplying graphic art. I hope I have convinced the reader that it is also and undoubtedly one of the most interesting media of aesthetic expression and, now that it has gained complete freedom, not likely to fall into neglect or disuse.

Xylography, whether on soft wood or on hard wood, or on a substitute such as linoleum, will grow in favour as artists discover the splendid training it is capable of giving, not only to the hand in the matter of execution, but also, and perhaps even more, to the mind in the matter of design. Material and tool enforce concentration. Experienced wood engravers of the old type confirm the fact that it is far more difficult to cut wood in the new and apparently so much cruder manner, precisely because every incision has a significance of its own which must be carefully premeditated and gauged beforehand ; scribbles and " accidents " which look so well in etching or water colour are here impossible. On the other hand, the material has more character than the lithographic stone, not to mention its substitutes.

Whether it deserves to exist as a means of decorating books that is another question which is open, I think, to legitimate doubt. It seems, however, quite likely that for spontaneous and forcible appeal it may come once more into general use in connection with posters, newspapers and modernised " broadsides." Portraits, such as Gallien's [144], already used extensively in continental periodicals, and satires,

244

such as Ludovic Rodo's "Duke of Marlborough" [74], are capital examples of this kind of thing; they are so much more personal than a mechanically reproduced design. Properly handled, woodcuts have a quality which Charles Ricketts has very aptly called "warmth," generated by the resistance which tools and materials oppose to the designer's will. Hence there is always a sense of intimacy in its products which pleases or vexes, that is to say stimulates, the beholder's mind to a much greater extent than any other form of print making.

To the collector, therefore, the woodcut offers happier hunting grounds than any other multiplying medium; but it demands also more aesthetic sensibility and intelligent discrimination. Technical standards of craftsmanship, on which so many collectors rely, are here of very little avail. The modern woodcutters share the privileges of the "monks" of Medmenham Abbey; they too may do as they wish, with only this single proviso: they must succeed. This is precisely the point where the difficulty for the collector arises: who is to tell him? He cannot take the artist's word or the world would be full of masterpieces; it may even happen that where the critic perceives success, the artist himself would pronounce failure.

In the ultimate resort the collector, like the rest of us, must rely, pending the last, on his own judgment.

BIBLIOGRAPHY OF BOOKS CONSULTED

BEEDHAM, J.: Wood Engraving. Ditchling, 1920.

BEWICK: Thomas Bewick's Works, Memorial Edition. London, 1885.

BINYON, Laurence: A Catalogue of Japanese and Chinese Woodcuts in the British Museum.

BURGER, Fritz: Einführung in die Moderne Kunst. Berlin, 1917.

CRAWHALL, J.: Old ffrendes wyth new faces with sutable sculpture, 1883. Chapbook Chaplets, 1884.

DALZIEL: The Brothers Dalziel. A record of fifty years' work. London, 1901.

DODGSON, Campbell: Woodcuts of the XV. Century in the John Ryland Library, Manchester. Manchester, 1915.

DODGSON, Campbell: Catalogue of Early German and Flemish Woodcuts in the British Museum. London, 1903.

FLETCHER, F. Morley: Woodblock Printing. London, 1916.

FRIEDLAENDER, Max J.: Der Holzschnitt. Berlin, 1921.

FUCHS, E.: Honoré Daumier, Munich, 1918.

FURST, Herbert: The Modern Woodcut, Print Collector's Quarterly, vol. 8, Nos. 2 and 3. London, 1921.

FURST, Herbert: Modern Woodcutters. Edited by
1. Gwendolen Raverat—Preface by H.F.
2. Frank Brangwyn—Preface by H.F.
3. T. Sturge Moore—Preface by Cecil French.
4. Edward Wadsworth—Preface by R. O. Drey.
London, 1919.

GAUGUIN, Paul: By De Rotonchamp. Weimar, 1906.

GAUGUIN, Paul: Thieme, Allgemeines Lexicon der Bildenden Künste. Leipzig, 1920.

GLASER, Curt: Munch. Berlin, 1918.

GUIDE to the Processes and Schools of Engraving. British Museum. London, 1914.

GUIDE to an Exhibition of Woodcuts and Metal-cuts of the XV. Century, chiefly of the German School. British Museum, 1914.

HUGO, The Rev. Thomas: Bewick's Woodcuts. London, 1866.

HAYDEN, Arthur: Chats on Old Prints. London, 1907.

JACKSON & CHATTO: A Treatise of Wood Engraving. London, 1861.

KRISTELLER, Paul: Kupferstich und Holzschnitt in vier Jahrhunderten. Berlin, 1921.

KURTH, Julius: Der Japanische Holzschnitt. Munich, 1922.

MEIER-GRAEFE, J.: Felix Vallotton. Paris, 1898.

SAHLEN, A.: Om Träsnilt och Träsnidari. Stockholm, 1914.

SALAMAN, Malcolm: The Modern Colour Print of original design. London, 1919.

SALAMAN, Malcolm: Modern Woodcuts and Lithographs. By British and French Artists. Studio Special Number. London, 1919.

WEITENKAMPF, F.: Wood Engraving To-day. New York, 1917.

WESTHEIM, Paul: Das Holzschnittbuch. Potsdam, 1921.

WHITMAN-SALAMAN: The Print Collector's Handbook. London, 1912.

WÜRTTEMBERGER, Ernst: Zeichnung, Holzschnitt und Illustration. Basel, 1919.

PERIODICALS, CURRENT AND DEFUNCT, CONTAINING WOODCUTS BY MODERN ARTISTS

The Apple. London, 1920-21.

L'Amour de l'Art. Paris.

Byblis, Miroir des Arts du Livre et de l'Estampe. Paris.

Der Blaue Reiter. Berlin.

Broom. Florence—Berlin.

The Dial. Edited by Charles Shannon and Charles Ricketts. London, 1893.

Eroica. Edited by Ettore Cozzani. La Spezia, 1910.

Form. London, 1921.

Genius. Berlin.

Hobby Horse. Century Guild. 1883.

L'Image. Paris, 1897.

The Golden Hind. London, 1922.

The Mask. Florence.

Mittheilungen der Vereinigung Bildender Künstler Oesterreichs : Ver Sacrum. 1903, Vienna.

Montparnasse. Paris, 1923.

Le Nouvel Imagier. Paris, 1914.

The Page. Edited by Gordon Craig.

The Play Boy. New York, 1919.

Der Sturm. Berlin, 1923.

HINTS ON THE PRACTICE OF XYLOGRAPHY

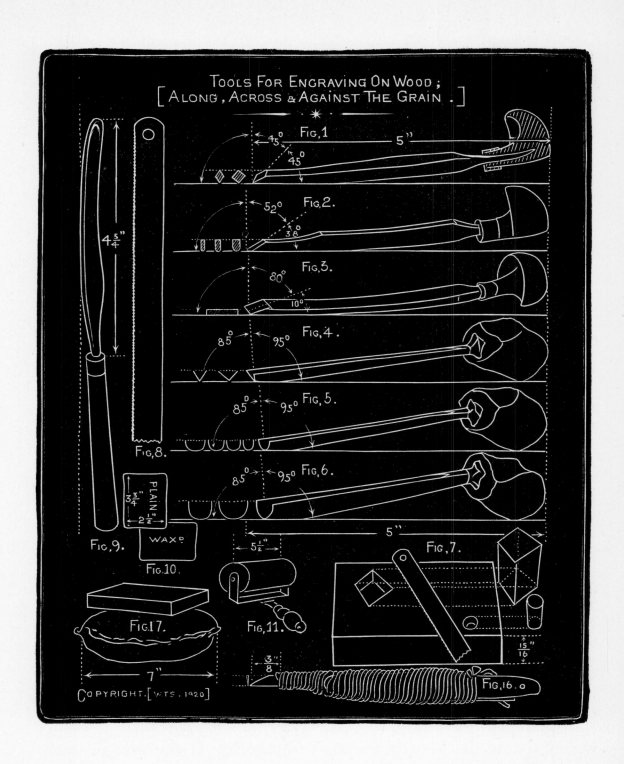

TOOLS FOR ENGRAVING ON WOOD;
[ALONG, ACROSS & AGAINST THE GRAIN.]

250

HINTS ON THE PRACTICE OF XYLOGRAPHY: BY W. THOMAS SMITH, DEMONSTRATOR IN WOOD ENGRAVING IN THE SLADE SCHOOL OF FINE ARTS, UNIVERSITY OF LONDON

I.

The Wood Engraver's "White Line" : Introduction.

The most spontaneous manifestations of the art of xylography are produced by what is called the wood engraver's " White Line " in contradistinction to the copper-plate engraver's and woodcutter's black one.

It is necessary at the outset to emphasize the technical importance of this " White Line," on which creative original work depends, for two reasons :

In the first place, it is the natural and, therefore, a speedy, economical and spontaneous one, which produces its effects at least six times faster than the woodcutter's " black " line.

Secondly, it is aesthetically superior, because of the singular and characteristic quality it gives to the print.

The method proceeds as nature itself does, evolving light from out of the darkness, a principle that differentiates wood engraving, in a fundamental way, from all other methods of producing prints by means of lines.

The exploration of this unique domain of the wood engraver, more particularly for original work, practically ceased about 1830, with the small subjects of Bewick, Clennell, Blake, Calvert and others, who regarded wood engraving not merely as a process for imitating something else, *e.g.*, reproducing a drawing, a menial use into which it had since their time fallen. They looked upon it as the objective sought for, *i.e.*, the original itself, a work that had to depend on aesthetic qualities which the tool and the material (the medium) would enable the knowledge and individuality of the draughtsman, the Painter-engraver, to give to it.

II.

The Wood Engraver's "White Line" v. The Copper-Plate Engraver's and Woodcutter's "Black Line" demonstrated.

As a demonstration of the foregoing principle of the white line take respectively a blackboard, a sheet of white paper, a piece of white and a piece of black chalk; regard both the black and the white chalk as the burin that will plough a line or furrow which would print white on the wood block, but black on the copper-plate.

The blackboard represents the wood block, and the white paper the copper (or some other metal) plate.

Set up some object for study, for instance, a pot of flowers, then proceed to render the drawing and effect of the arrangement, first on the white paper with black lines, etc., and then depict it on the blackboard, with various white lines, dots, dashes and spaces.

The latter (minus of course the clear incisive white line, which the burin alone can give), will suffice to indicate the principle, the true *modus operandi* of the wood engraver, the former, that of all other forms of pure engraving on metal, excepting only the ancient metal white line work sometimes mistaken for wood engraving, but which is of no use where spontaneity of expression is essential.

By means of this simple exercise, it will be realized that the ability to engrave on both materials (metal and wood) equally well, turns solely on the ability to handle the burin (on, of course, a smaller scale), as easily as the chalks, etc. (on the larger one).

The work of my pupils (some in this book) has proved that this is no more difficult to acquire than wielding a pen was, when first we set out to render pot hooks and hangers.

In the light of present-day developments of it in both Europe and America, it is obvious that the possibilities of wood engraving have never been fully examined; further, that its development was handicapped and restricted by the exigences of reproductive work, which unfortunately monopolized it.

Until comparatively recently, wood engraving *par excellence* also came to consist largely of how close or minutely one could engrave, *i.e.* cut, white lines, side by side, with a more or less mechanical regularity, reproducing various tints which, with but few reservations, were of a cast-iron or photographic quality.

The more accomplished, because bolder, work of this order, with some exceptions to be found among the engravers of Doré (Pisan for

252

instance), reminded one of engine turning or machine ruling; in fact, special tools were introduced for this kind of work; they were graded and numbered, usually from one to twelve, and so on, their conception, as well as their use, except in some rare cases, displaying the mind of the engineer rather than that of the artist.

III.

Tools (Burins and Scoupers): The principle of their construction and method of sharpening.

But three kinds of tools are required for both wood engraving and wood cutting, namely, the square Burin, and lozenge-shaped, and the Scouper, see Figs. 1 and 2.

Fig. 13.   Fig. 14.

These implements every engraver has to make up (from the rough state in which they are sold) to his or her own liking and requirements. The cutting power of the burin is at its best when ground and set at half a right angle, *i.e.*, 45 degrees : if the angle is more, it does not cut so easily or smoothly, if less, the point becomes too attenuated, and is, therefore, liable to break off under the strain put upon it.
The angle of the scouper, a tool made stouter throughout, may, therefore, be reduced to about 38 degrees with advantage to its cutting qualities.
The keel of the tool should be straight from heel to the toe or cutting

point when viewed from underneath, Fig. 13, and slightly curved when seen from the side, Fig. 1, so that when raising its handle, and simultaneously driving the tool in any direction, its point will sink (dive) into and cut the wood to the required depth. The varying depths, owing to the angular shape of the burin, will also dictate the varying widths of the (white) line required.

On the other hand, if the handle be depressed whilst the burin is simultaneously pushed forward this action will cause the cutting point to dive up again, so to speak, out of the wood.

This narrows this incised line more or less gradually or abruptly, according to the way the depression of its handle is regulated : were the burin not so curved, suavity or fluency of line would be impossible.

Fig. 12.

These tools are sharpened as shown in Fig. 14, on an oilstone ; "Arkansas hard," " Turkey " or " Charnwood Forest," being the best kinds.

The handles of the tools must be shaped and pitched as in Figs. 1, 2, 3. They are set, so as to give adequate clearance for the hand gripping them, as shown in Figs. 12, 13 and 14, enabling the point of the burin to cut as described, to travel over any part of the wood block or metal plate, which is best held in place on a leather bag during this operation. This bag, stuffed with silver sand, Fig. 17, serves not only as a rest, but also as a pivot on which to turn the block or plate.

Having decided on a subject for engraving, a piece of prepared apple, pear or box wood is procured the size the print is to be. As the wood is a section of the tree about an inch thick, the cutting, therefore, will be against (*i.e.*, on the end of) the grain, not along and across it as in wood plank engraving and cutting.

254

IV.

Commencing an Engraving on Wood: Six Alternative Methods.

There are usually six alternative ways of commencing an engraving (other methods with experience and enterprise will suggest themselves).

First, one may black the surface of the wood, with for instance, Indian ink, thus making a small blackboard of it on which may be indicated the proportions of the composition in faintly cut or scratched lines, which will of course be white, no other kind of preliminary drawing on the wood being resorted to.

Secondly, some sketching may be done on the wood with a lead pencil; the lines of which reflecting light on its blackened surface as they do, can then be gone over (and more or less revised when cut into) with the burin.

The effect produced by these lines (white) will, of course, be shown by the light colour of the wood, as its blackened surface is cut away. This method may be pursued when engraving either direct from nature or from sketches; it permits of a quality, style and individuality that is not to be obtained by other methods; obviously, it is a procedure that requires more experience and confidence than the others.

If one desires to proceed more cautiously, a preliminary sketch with an ordinary pen and some writing ink may be made on the surface of the wood, which absorbs the ink quickly and indelibly, or the wood may be whitened with some flake white powder and a little water, a little brick dust powder being added to give the polished surface of the wood a tooth for the pencil.

The wood being thus prepared, the design can then be drawn on the block (a good 6H pencil is best), with or without additional tones or washes made of the writing ink, diluted with water as required, put on with a sable brush.

One may alternatively paint the design on the block in body colour, *i.e.*, with Chinese white and Indian ink with water, but not too thickly, otherwise it will flake off in patches when the burin cuts through it into the wood, and so perchance carry away some important detail in the drawing, before it has been secured in gravure with the burin.

Lastly, the subject, whether a painting or a drawing, may be photographed on the wood.

Whichever way one decides to proceed with the subject it should always be kept in mind that the quality and effect aimed at in the wood engraving is to be produced by long or short *white* lines, spaces, etc., aided, but not trammelled, by any of the foregoing preliminaries, some or all of which are probably in black lines.

It should be realized at the outset, that all the resulting black spaces, *i.e.*, the wood left between these white lines as they are cut by the burin or scouper, are to be regarded (if at all) as more or less accidental, so to speak, just as the reverse is the case with metal engraving.

These (engraved and, therefore), " white lines " will necessarily be suggested by the requirements of the subject; their varying directions and qualities (thick and thin; straight flowing or broken) will render the modelling and the more or less broken luminous tones required, relieved by black and white spaces judiciously left on the one hand, and cut away on the other, with the scouper, or if the space be a large one, with a gouge and mallet.

V.

Proving and Printing without a Press, viz., by Hand, with the Burnisher and Frotton.

The medium and practice of wood engraving fortunately is not dependent on mechanical aid or assistance, and the less these are resorted to the better the quality of the limited edition of prints will be. The most brilliant proofs, such as would be required by some collectors, are those taken by hand, *i.e.*, with the burnisher and frotton, with the best quality proofing ink, on the best quality paper of a suitable tone, in the following manner.

A piece of (for instance) India paper, of a requisite thickness, depending on taste and the size of the print is laid face downwards on the engraved block which has been inked with the roller, Fig. 11; a thin smooth card, Fig. 10, is then rubbed over the paper, causing it to adhere, stick evenly to the inked block; a second card charged with beeswax is then rubbed over it; lubricated in this way by the wax, it will not rough up under friction.

The first card is again rubbed over the paper in conjunction with a steel (Fig. 9), ivory or bone burnisher placed on top of it; some pressure of course is required when doing this.

256

"Vigilantia." Trial proof (fragment), much reduced. For particulars see p. 261-2.

By this ancient method of the " niello " workers a fine brilliant impression may be taken, because the varying degrees of pressure required, greater on the darker parts in the engraving, are thereby better regulated than is possible by the mechanism, the press of the printer and his system called "overlaying." These " overlays " are various patterns of paper cut out by the machine minder to correspond in shape with the darker masses in the engraved block, and stuck on the " tympan," *i.e.*, that part of his press that folds over on to the paper to be printed on; the latter is placed between it and the block.

For limited editions of more than say twenty-five prints, or for engravings of a large area, one would probably prefer the printer to make the impressions and by overlaying, if necessary, as near as possible to the artist's burnished proof.

Nevertheless, no impression can compare for quality of surface, etc., with the proof carefully taken by one moderately skilful in the use of the burnisher and the frottons, *i.e.*, the two cards in this case, Fig. 10.

VI.

Alterations and Repairs to a Woodcut or Engraving: How they are made.

Accidents, corrections and revisions to a wood block are effected by making incisions and then inserting plugs, *i.e.*, pieces of the same kind of wood, or by rubbing down and so lowering the surface, with fine glass paper or by both combined, thus darkening the subject. This glass paper, however, must be used with discretion, or much needless work, in re-entering, *i.e.*, going again into the incised lines with the burin to widen (to lighten) them again may ensue. The black spaces between the white lines (*i.e.*, the surfaces, which of course supply the ink to the print), are pyramidical in section, and a scraper or fine glass paper applied evenly all over them, therefore, lowers and so widens them, at the same time narrowing the " white line " and causing the block to print a darker tone.

Plugging, up to a moderate area, for many reasons is best done by the engraver himself, in the following manner :

If area for correction be small, drill a hole where required, cut, trim and then taper a piece of wood (the plug) as round as possible (with the flat tool, Fig. 3) to fit the hole, Fig. 7.

258

Should a plug of irregular shape be required, cut and shape the plug first of all, tapering it on every side; this done, hold the smaller end (which is to be inserted) to the block, exactly covering the surface to be repaired; now scratch a line on the block close up to, round the plug, with an ordinary fine needle, thus the area and shape of the hole required for the plug will be indicated and made to correspond exactly to the plug prepared for it.

Next cut into these scratches lines (making them deeper) with the burin and scouper, keeping the sides of the resulting hole or pit upright; this would be about a $\frac{1}{4}$ inch deep if the area of the plug is about $\frac{1}{2}$ an inch square.

Apply some powdered resin to the sides of this pit and also to the sides of the plug itself.

Now insert it, and then, with a hammer, drive the plug into the pit. The block should be resting on some flat, heavy, hard surface meanwhile.

By this means the taper-shaped piece of wood is forced, squeezed on to the side of the pit, more particularly at the surface edges, the place that matters most; a close fit all round is thus ensured, the resin securely cements it there and prevents its springing or coming out again, Fig. 7.

Next take a sheet of thin card or thick paper, and an engineer's hack saw (thirty-two teeth to the inch), cut a hole in the card or paper, and lay it on the block to protect it, allowing the unwanted end of the plug (*i.e.*, the part above the surface of the block), to stick through this hole in the card or paper. Now lay the saw (the blade only, no handle is required—Figs. 7 and 8) flat on the card protecting the block. Then cut off this projecting part by sawing evenly all round, gradually working towards the centre; if sawn through from one side direct to the other it is liable to chip off at the edge and so spoil the operation. The remainder of the inserted plug that still projects is then carefully pared down, fairly close to the level of the whole surface of the block, with a small sharp chisel called a flat tool set in a wood engraver's handle, Fig. 3, working from the outside edge of the plug towards its centre.

The inserted wood is then levelled off perfectly flush with the finest glass paper (known as 00 and Flour) and finally polished by rubbing with a piece of fine brown paper, free from dust or grit, all held stretched across something flat whilst in use.

To revise large areas it is advisable to send the block to the maker.

VII.

Woodcuts and Engravings along and across the grain, made either with the knife and gouge or with the scrive and gouge.

Wood cutting on the plank is done either with a scrive (*i.e.*, a hollow burin), Fig. 4, or a knife, Fig. 16, assisted by gouges of different widths. When the knife is used, two cuts are required to the scrive's one; the latter, therefore, is quicker.

The small thin blade of a pocket knife, partly bound with string, Fig. 16, to protect the fingers and as a grip (if made of good steel) is as good as the knives made and sold for this purpose.

The first cut is made along each side of the line, *i.e.*, the wood to be left standing, which must be pyramidical in section.

Fig. 15.

The knife when cutting is tilted to one side, at an angle of (approx.) 45 degrees, as in Fig. 15.

Another cut is then made, more or less parallel to the first cut (depending on requirements), at a distance of from about $\frac{1}{32}$ of an inch upwards, the knife tilted (the 45 degrees in the opposite direction). These cuts made at opposite angles, therefore, cause a Vee-shaped strip of wood, automatically, to come away from each side of the line, leaving a right angle furrow on both sides of the wood left standing, which will, therefore, print black; the superfluous wood between these trenches is then removed with a sharp gouge.

It will thus be seen that to get a single black line, by this art craft of the " Form Schneider," four cuts are required with the knife but only two with the scrive.

The scrive is better known as a wood carver's Vee or parting tool. For engravings and woodcuts it is ground, set and pitched at a

"Diffidentia." Trial proof (fragment), much reduced. This and "Vigilantia," p. 257,
were demonstrations of freehand *plank* engraving by the writer made with "*the scrive*."
The surface of the wood was first blackened all over, hence the tool acted in a similar
way to a piece of chalk on a blackboard. See remarks on next page.

261

different angle to that of the wood carver, as invented and used by the writer, and, as shown in Fig. 4, with handles of cork.

It may thus be pushed in exactly the same way on soft woods, as the solid burin or scouper is used on the hard ones.

Unlike the latter, however, it is not so easy to sharpen or keep in order. When in good trim the " scrive " cuts quickly, with ease, and as sharply and cleanly across the grain of the wood as with (*i.e.*, along) it. With the additional aid of a few gouges of different widths (Figs. 5 and 6), the scrive is not only suitable for woodcuts, but, eminently so, for wood engravings, especially on a comparatively large scale, when speed and ease of expression are more than ever necessary ; as, for instance, when engraving a head or a portrait direct from life, see examples (reduced) pages 257 and 261, trial pieces of two prints at B.M. and V.A.M. freehand work, with the scrive and gouges, evolved from sketches from life reversed in a mirror.

VIII.

Wood (the species used) for Engraving, etc.,
along and across the grain.

Any soft even grained wood is suitable for woodcuts and engravings made on the plank (*i.e.*, along and across the grain), for instance, well-seasoned cherry, lime, maple, sycamore and American white wood.

Planks of such wood of various widths, 1 inch thick, are planed flat and then smoothed with a scraper or glass paper.

Cut or engraved on with knife, scrive or gouge, both sides being made use of, they also yield good colour prints in oil, and delicate fine ones in water colours, *i.e.*, to those who know the proper papers to use and the Japanese method of printing them.

IX.

Strength or boldness of line in scale with the size of the print:
a guide (approx.) to determining this.

Some help as to what strength of line to adopt in an engraving may be found in an old tradition to the effect that the print which best emits all the qualities it is capable of, is of a requisite boldness, not, however, too coarse or harsh in texture. Mere fineness, on the other hand, like much smooth painting, is too often a refuge for incompetence.

This tradition and theory (one easily tested) is as follows : At a distance of three times the diagonal (*i.e.*, of the length from left bottom to right top corner of the print), the lines, dots, dashes in the darker, the shadows or semi-transparent parts of the subject, should still be just visible ; and only on increasing this distance should these lines, etc., merge into half-tones, etc. A less strength or boldness of line than this results in a diminution of the required vibrant qualities, transparency, or luminosity in those parts of the print.

X.

The Necessity for Tuition and Guidance.

Wood engraving, *i.e.*, in its best sense, cannot of course be learnt from books or articles such as this, although it is hoped that these hints will assist the adoption of correct methods based on sound principles.

For instance, one gives the diagrams, Figs. 12, 13 and 14, showing how the burin must be held if one is to excel in using it freely, but it is not possible to explain how it should be driven and controlled, ocular demonstration is necessary ; similar remarks apply to using the burnisher and frottons.

Without tuition at the start, one courts bad habits, difficult to eradicate, unnecessary set backs, tool difficulties, involving much loss of time ; a requisite confidence and the facility necessary to express oneself freely is impaired, the technique, quality and fluency of line suffers. All this results in undue limitations of the medium.

These limitations, usually, are evident in a dearth (if not entire absence) of line, half-tones or light, often with too great a predominance of black in the print, or a predilection for dark subjects, night scenes, sombre interiors or miniature poster work of the contrasting black and white order.

XI.

Conclusion: the secret of Wood Engraving, as with any other art, consists in allowing the medium to dictate its technique.

In conclusion, it should be stated that these hints on the practice of

263

xylography are based on the chief points made at a lecture which the writer was encouraged by Professor Tonks, F.R.C.S. and others, at University College, to give three years ago to art students interested in wood engraving. It pretends, therefore, to nothing more than an introduction to the subject, and in particular to the new application of its principle : this may be referred to as the rediscovery of the use of a *white line working on black*, the principle followed in many of the examples in this book, which, obviously enough, must have been engraved by draughtsmen, who *can* draw, paint, etch or model.

Some of these examples, as the writer happens to know, demonstrate the fact that a long novitiate is not necessary to acquire this art.

With adequate instruction at the start a draughtsman invariably uses a burin with distinction, and always with increasing facility, *i.e.*, speed and precision.

The secret of this undoubtedly consists, of course, in permitting the burin and the material on which it operates to dictate the technique, aided only, but not trammelled as it used to be, by lines (black or white) drawn on the wood, which must be regarded as purely preparatory.

Hence modern " wood engraving " rightly avoids the undesirable (not to say unnatural) strain put on the medium by what used to be called " facsimile work," the art of the " Form Schneider," that of " the sixties " referred to.

To freedom from this arbitrary restraint of reproduction which the genius of Bewick and others thrived on, is due the charm and distinction of the print known as an original wood engraving and the consequent revival and expansion of a well-nigh extinct art.

THE END

264

INDEX OF
WOODCUTTERS AND ENGRAVERS

PP

265

266

268

GENERAL INDEX

269

270

271